"Here's America's Unquietest Library

Salt Lake City Public Library

SALT LAKE CITY, UTAH (1999–2003)

The Salt Lake City Public Library comprises a five-story, triangular-shaped main building housing book stacks and reading rooms; an adjacent rectangular administrative structure; and a glass-enclosed, crescent-shaped internal street of shops and restaurants conceived as an "Urban Room." These structures are complemented by rooftop gardens with views of the surrounding Wasatch Mountain Range and an outdoor plaza with fountains and an amphitheater.

Gus Powell photographed the library between June 22 and June 24, 2007, during the Utah Arts Festival, an annual arts event showcasing musicians, dancers, filmmakers, storytellers, visual artists, and poets. His photographs not only capture dramatic visual links between different functions and scales that are created by the structures' glass walls, open stairways, and balconies, but they also demonstrate Moshe Safdie's ability to create buildings that foster a dynamic and communal urbanism.

New York-based photographer Gus Powell regularly contributes to *The New Yorker* magazine. A book of his photographs was published under the title *The Company of Strangers* in 2003.

Crystal Bridges Museum of American Art
Bentonville, Arkansas

Skirball Cultural Center
Los Angeles, California

Scala Arts Publishers, Inc.
New York

GLOBAL
THE ARCHIT
MOSHE

Donald Albrecht

with essays by

Sarah Williams Goldhagen

and Moshe Safdie

CITIZEN
ECTURE OF
SAFDIE

First published in 2010 by
Crystal Bridges Museum of American Art
Bentonville, Arkansas
www.crystalbridges.org

in association with

Scala Arts Publishers, Inc.
141 Wooster Street, Suite 4D
New York, NY 10012
www.scalapublishers.com

This revised edition published in 2015

Published on the occasion of the exhibition
Global Citizen: The Architecture of Moshe Safdie,
curated by Donald Albrecht

Exhibition Schedule
October 8, 2010–January 14, 2011
National Gallery of Canada
Ottawa, Ontario, Canada

October 13, 2012–January 28, 2013
*Moshe Safdie: The Path to Crystal Bridges
(Selections from* Global Citizen*)*
Crystal Bridges Museum of American Art
Bentonville, Arkansas

October 19, 2013–March 2, 2014
Skirball Cultural Center
Los Angeles, California

May 31, 2014–September 2, 2014
Crystal Bridges Museum of American Art
Bentonville, Arkansas

September 10, 2015–January 10, 2016
National Academy Museum
New York, New York

February 15, 2016–May 13, 2016
BSA Space, Boston Society of Architects
Boston, Massachusetts

Creating a Sense of Place

My first experience of Crystal Bridges was of a construction project rising from a heavily wooded and steep landscape. The site features several intersecting ravines carved into the Ozark foothills. The museum is built where shifting streams feed the lower Mississippi River watershed across the northern tier of Arkansas and southern Missouri. The location is very near to where the Cherokee's Trail of Tears came to a bitter pause before finally coming to rest in Oklahoma Indian territory, just west of Bentonville.

The museum is only a few blocks from the town's historic square where Sam Walton's original "Five and Ten" store has been preserved and where a monument honors Confederate Civil War soldiers, some of whom camped on the museum site after being routed by Union troops at the Battle of Pea Ridge nearby. Alice Walton and her brothers grew up surrounded by these woods and "hollers," literally in her family's back yard. It is a special place, as she often says. The ways in which these histories intersect—local, regional, national, and natural—inform this remarkable new museum.

Crystal Bridges is named for nearby Crystal Springs that is a source for a stream running under the museum's "bridges." These meandering intersections of art, history, and nature flowing out of and into each other are visually paraphrased in Moshe Safdie's architecture for this museum with its rootedness in the land and the community it is now transforming.

In my experience, very few museums are so perfectly tuned to their purpose and place. Moshe Safdie's work in this regard, and for many other reasons, is exceptional. Over the past half century, he has envisioned and built some of the most memorable places of our time. Many of the architect's most ambitious projects have been built outside the United States and Canada and, therefore, exist somewhat outside the view of North American audiences. This exhibition is, in part, an attempt to examine Safdie's work in its broader international context and to celebrate his unique vision. In many of his projects over the past several decades, Safdie has designed buildings that not only reflect but actively participate in, energize, and even drive the very purposes for which they have been created.

Mounting an architecture exhibition is comparable to designing a museum. It is a creative enterprise employing diverse talents, craftsmanship, and hard work. We thank exhibition curator and catalogue editor, Donald Albrecht. The award-winning Office dA designed the overall exhibition, and Pure+Applied were the project's graphic designers. Their designs complement and comment on Safdie's architecture in telling ways. We are grateful to Sarah Williams Goldhagen whose catalogue essay locates the multifaceted, multinational sources and spirit of Safdie's global citizenship. We especially thank Moshe's wife, Michal Ronnen Safdie, an internationally recognized artist in her own right, who provided several recent photographs for this publication and the exhibition. We are likewise indebted to several other architectural photographers, especially Arkansas-based Timothy Hursley. Our deepest gratitude goes to Moshe Safdie and the entire staff at Safdie Architects. Friendship and gratitude extend, as well, to our gracious partners and mentors in this enterprise, the Skirball Cultural Center, an organization that ably demonstrates our own mission to establish an open, diverse, community-oriented institution. We are especially grateful to Skirball founding president and chief executive officer, Uri D. Herscher, and his able team, including Robert Kirschner, museum director, and Kathryn Girard, chief of staff. It was our good fortune that Moshe Safdie was the architect whose design for the Skirball captures and embodies so much of what we hope to achieve in Bentonville, Arkansas, as Crystal Bridges Museum of American Art becomes a reality.

Don Bacigalupi, Ph.D.
Board Member and Former Executive Director, Crystal Bridges Museum of American Art

An Extraordinary Journey

This publication celebrates more than four decades of Moshe Safdie's extraordinary journey as an architect. I have been a part of this journey for more than three decades and continue to admire firsthand the principles and values that guide his work. Each of his projects has been different from the others, but all have been inspired by Moshe Safdie's genius and gentle sensibility.

I first met Moshe in Jerusalem in the mid-1970s. I was then the executive vice president of the four-campus Hebrew Union College, and Moshe had recently been asked to plan the expansion of our Jerusalem campus. I was impressed by his contextual approach to designing our academic and cultural complex in the heart of the city of Jerusalem. Moshe and I soon became, and have remained, close friends and colleagues. It certainly helped that both of us were born in Israel, spoke the same language, were close in age, and shared many of the same formative experiences. We formed a bond of trust and caring that has strengthened and deepened with time.

By 1983 the idea for the Skirball Cultural Center in Los Angeles had emerged. It was envisioned as a cultural village dedicated to exploring the connections between 4,000 years of Jewish heritage and American democratic ideals. I was elated that Moshe and I would have the opportunity to collaborate again in shaping this new vision. I had always thought that you hired an architect and then, if you liked what he or she proposed and could afford it, you moved ahead. Working with Moshe proved to be a very different experience. He was a vital part of the Skirball's planning team, contributing as much to the shaping of the institutional mission as to the buildings that would give it form.

The parcel we had acquired in Los Angeles was a onetime refuse dump bordered by the steep hillsides of the Santa Monica Mountains. It might not have seemed that promising a site to some architects, but Moshe was undeterred. I remember him saying, "This site has many secrets which I must discover." He talked about how outdoor spaces could become "living rooms" of the Center, and how such a setting could engage and embrace all who visit. Moshe likened the design process to producing fine wine, where the passage of time serves to mature, shape, and refine the vintage. Fourteen years after the Skirball's public opening, that dynamic process continues to flourish. As we enter our fourth and fifth phases of construction, we see before us a superbly realized complex of buildings, courtyards, and gardens, a seamless integration of a holistic architectural vision.

Moshe often says that clients get what they deserve from their architects. Buildings are only as good as their clients are purposeful, conscientious, persistent, and clear about what they hope to achieve. To the Skirball Cultural Center's aspirations, Moshe Safdie has given voice and character. Such a gift transcends the realm of architecture: it speaks to, and lifts high, the human spirit.

Uri D. Herscher
Founding president and chief executive officer, Skirball Cultural Center
Los Angeles, California

CREATING A HUMANIST ARCHITECTURE

Donald Albrecht

"Here's America's Unquietest Library," *USA Today* announced in October 2003, upon the opening of the Salt Lake City Public Library. Designed by Moshe Safdie, the project defined a new type of library as a center of civic activity. "Salt Lake City," the newspaper continued, "Leads the Way in a New Vision."[1] While libraries have historically served varied community functions, this library has expanded the notion: it was conceived as an inclusive alternative to the city's more exclusive Mormon institutions, while the library itself is only one component of a lively urban ensemble. Book stacks, reading rooms, and private study carrels flow seamlessly onto a soaring, crescent-shaped internal street of shops and restaurants, an outdoor plaza with fountains and an amphitheater, and rooftop gardens with views of nearby mountains. Walls of glass create dramatic visual interpenetrations between diverse functions, scales, and moods, realizing Safdie's intention to use architecture not only to express, but also to generate, open engagement in community life.

Salt Lake City's library, however, represents just one expression of Safdie's commitment to a humanistic modern architecture. Encompassing more than seventy-five completed buildings, communities, and master plans on three continents and an even greater number of projects and competition entries, his career has evolved in a series of distinct phases, each phase enriching his vocabulary and expanding his international impact. Safdie has traced a remarkable trajectory in the canon of modern architecture, from the 1960s when the twenty-nine-year-old architect designed Habitat, one of the century's most significant experiments in prefabricated housing, until today, when he practices within an ever-expanding global architectural culture. In parallel with his architectural practice, Safdie has also written eight books, authored dozens of articles, lectured internationally, and taught at major universities including McGill, Yale, and Harvard. Canada recently honored him with his own postage stamp, while two Safdie buildings in Tel Aviv—Israel's main airport and a research center named after Yitzhak Rabin—appear on Israeli stamps.

Safdie's most significant buildings have been commissioned for the public sphere. Designing museums, cultural centers, libraries, memorials, schools, and religious facilities, he has been an unapologetic proponent of architecture as a social, populist art. "Architecture and urbanism," Safdie has noted in relation to his work, "are not the same as other art forms, nor can meaningful architectural response to the making of our environment be 'in' one day and 'out' the next. A profession that affects the daily life of billions, where every line drawn and design created has economic, ecological, social, behavioral, psychological and spiritual impact, must work within the ethical framework that is open to serious debate. An ethical framework is not a fixed dictum; it must invite discourse."[2]

An avid polemicist, Safdie has certainly generated his share of discourse and debate. While he has been acclaimed by clients and the general public, he has been—and remains today—a controversial figure. For his proponents, Safdie's aesthetic language of transcendent light, powerful geometric form, and metaphoric imagery produces buildings that are ceremonial and uplifting, without being intimidating. His detractors see a different side. To a great extent, Safdie is an architect who creates

Moshe Safdie (right), his aunt,
and brother in Haifa, 1952

Moshe Safdie in St. Peter's Square,
Rome, 1953

buildings that resonate most powerfully with laypeople, and it is the very features that make them popular—their grand civic gestures, their iconographic legibility, their commitment to a contextual urbanism—that also render them targets of critics. To the latter, Safdie's grand forms seem bombastic, his contextual references ersatz, his metaphors too facile. Still, by consistently arguing for architecture to play a major role in people's lives, Safdie has carved a distinctive niche for himself in contemporary culture. Through his buildings, he has been especially adept at realizing the aspirations of a surprisingly diverse group of clients, including New England patricians; Indian Sikhs; and the governments of Israel, Canada, and the United States. For them, he has created buildings where communities are forged of strangers, memory is enshrined, and identity is created in built form. Speaking of his controversial public library in Vancouver, Canada, Safdie has said, "When a building is that popular and well-loved, the least the critics can do is reconcile that affection with what they think is wrong with it."[3]

"THE SHAPE OF THINGS TO COME"

Raised in the Middle East, Safdie is not new to conflict and controversy. He was born in 1938 in Haifa, the ancient Mediterranean port city that was then in Palestine but became part of Israel after the country's founding following the 1948 Arab-Israeli War. Jewish immigration, primarily from Europe during the early decades of the twentieth century, had, by 1945, transformed the city's overwhelmingly Arab Muslim population into a heterogeneous mix of Muslims, Christians, and Jews. In Haifa the young Sadfie encountered a model of multiethnic globalism. The modernist terraced housing in which Safdie grew up would also exert a profound effect on his architectural sensibility.

In 1953, after Israel nationalized its textile industry (his father's profession), the Safdie family emigrated to Montreal, where Safdie enrolled in McGill University. He graduated in 1961 with an undergraduate thesis project for "A Three-Dimensional Modular Building System," which laid the theoretical and design groundwork for his Habitat series of housing projects developed in the mid-1960s. Safdie's thesis was intellectually grounded in his report entitled "Some Aspects of Housing in North America," based on firsthand observations he made during a tour of numerous cities.[4] The first of Safdie's many publications to parallel his architecture, this booklet's drawings and photos compared various residential schemes from high-rise public housing projects in Chicago to mid-rise townhouses in Detroit and low-rise homes in suburban San Francisco. To Safdie, the suburban projects squandered land and resources, while the urban ones lacked privacy and gardens. His thesis proposed an alternative to both. The report also demonstrated Safdie's capacity for intense research, as well as his commitment to housing and to architecture as a social art, all evident at an early age.

While few students ever see their thesis projects realized, Safdie achieved this extraordinary accolade when the Canadian government accepted his project as a pavilion for the upcoming international Expo '67. This seminal project—Habitat—launched the first phase of Safdie's work, which continued into the early 1970s. Safdie was at the time a young modernist committed to pure geometric forms and to the ability of industrialized building systems to improve people's lives. His projects, animated by circulation systems such as skywalks, elevators, and stairways, created what Safdie called "three-dimensional communities."[5] Safdie was drawing from the experimental nature and social trends of the 1960s and looking to the work of the Metabolists—Japanese architects who believed that the modern city would experience massive population increases and should be built of modular, expandable units. (Safdie compared this to the city growing organically like a shell.) His buildings of this period used repetitive grids and modules, creating structures of multiple functions and flexibility. They also represented sophisticated syntheses of architecture and landscape, featuring rooftop gardens and terraces that were integrated into the built forms.

Moshe Safdie working on his undergraduate thesis project, "A Three-Dimensional Modular Building System," McGill University, Montreal, ca. 1960

Safdie's aspiration for Habitat was to achieve the benefits of the suburban single-family home—its visual and acoustical privacy and its individual plot of land—at the lower cost per unit and more efficient land use of urban housing. A radical solution to the need for high-quality, affordable housing, Habitat was conceived as an apartment building that functioned as a city-within-the-city with residential units as well as community and cultural facilities and was constructed using industrialized materials and processes. It represented a landmark in the fields of housing design, modern architecture, and urban planning and provided an important starting point for Safdie's subsequent work in all three fields. Inspired by the hillside village of Haifa, yet also expressive of the experimental spirit of its time, Habitat employed a completely new structural system of stacked, prefabricated concrete boxes lifted into place by cranes. Also innovative were the complex's prefabricated bathrooms of molded fiberglass and its preassembled kitchens. Offering private entries similar to freestanding houses, Habitat's 158 units were accessed from Plexiglas-canopied pedestrian skywalks located on every fourth floor. By overlapping the boxes, the roof of one unit served as the garden terrace for the one above, showing Safdie's ability to create a contemporary architectural language from historic precedent.

All of these futuristic features generated international interest. Millions of people, including Charles de Gaulle and Indira Gandhi, toured Habitat, and television programs, newspapers, and magazines provided extensive coverage. The project was even the subject of cartoons: a milkman is unable to find the right apartment in Habitat's beehive design, a mother wonders how her son will hang his wash, and a child on the beach recreates its Lego-like configuration in sand. Writing in the *New York Times*, Ada Louise Huxtable acknowledged Habitat's problems—its high unit cost of more than $100,000, for example, since only one-sixth of the original scheme was built—but went on to praise its importance: "Montreal has an international landmark," she wrote, "and eventually 158 urban families will live just a little bit better than the rest of us. Both the puzzle and the promise of the future is in this housing."[6] For Safdie, only thirty-two years old, the excitement culminated in his appearance on the April 19, 1971, cover of *Newsweek* magazine behind a model of Habitat Puerto Rico and under the banner headline "The Shape of Things to Come."

Below
Moshe Safdie on cover of
Newsweek, April 19, 1971

Right
Habitat under construction,
Montreal, 1964–67

The *Newsweek* article came at the end of Safdie's attempts to replicate the Habitat model around the world. For New York City he designed two different schemes along Manhattan's East River in 1967–68. These were joined by Habitats for Puerto Rico (1968–70), Israel (1969–70), Rochester (1971), and Tehran (1976–78). His goal was to gain greater structural and circulation efficiencies and lower costs than at Habitat Montreal, and he developed a wide array of options in a short time frame. There were different module shapes, from rectangular to hexagonal and octahedral sections; variations in density (forty to three hundred units per acre); structural systems (load-bearing and cable-suspension); sites (flat and hilly); units with single-height, double-height, and split-level interiors; and building heights from two stories to fifty stories. Differing climactic conditions were also addressed. In his proposal for Habitat Israel, for example, Safdie designed units with rotating fiberglass domes that opened interiors to the outdoors, allowing residents to continue their local tradition of living in nature. These structures replicated and reinterpreted features of the area's historic architecture—an important and early manifestation of Safdie's trademark progressive contextualism—with a strategy that used modern construction techniques and technologies, while acknowledging local environmental conditions, materials, and forms. None of Safdie's efforts to build Habitat outside of Expo '67 was realized, however.[7] "Our technological ideas were naïve," Safdie said in 1990. "The mistake in Habitat was the idea of a closed system in which everything was to be made in the same factory," with a consequent lack of cost savings, on-time scheduling, and marketplace competition. In contrast, today's successful "open" manufacturing systems involve many companies using interchangeable parts from different makers.[8]

Despite never expanding beyond its original prototype, Habitat has nevertheless become highly prized housing in Montreal as well as an historic landmark. In 1986, more than two decades after

Habitat's arrival was greeted with critical acclaim but skepticism about whether people would actually want to live there, its renters purchased the complex and have since made considerable investments in improvements. At the same time, while Safdie, who still owns an apartment there, carefully oversees Habitat's exterior, tenants have added individual elements like awnings and plantings and have also customized their apartments in styles ranging from traditional to mid-century modern. "With Wear and Tear, Habitat Has Become a Home," a *New York Times* headline proclaimed in an article that, like so many others, accompanied a Habitat anniversary.[9] Ironically, however, Habitat, which was conceived as a utopian scheme for low-cost housing, is now only affordable to the upper-middle class. And, as only a fraction of the original plan was built—without any mixture of urban uses, Safdie's dream of a city-within-the-city was never realized.

The first phase of Safdie's career also comprised opportunities to reach beyond the residential scope of his Habitat concept toward the public and urban spheres of his later, mature career: the San Francisco State College Student Union proposal (1967–68) and the Centre Pompidou competition (1971). Conceived as a pedestrian transit hub at the center of a 20,000-student campus, the student union offered twenty-four-hour-a-day classrooms, stores, dining halls, and meeting areas in a beehive-like complex of angled, pre-cast concrete modules in which movable platforms allowed students to reconfigure the interior shapes of rooms. With two of the building's levels sunken into the ground and seven rising above in ziggurat profile, the student union's landscaped roofs, stairways, and landings seemed to grow organically out of the earth, offering dramatic contrast to its staid, boxy neighbors.

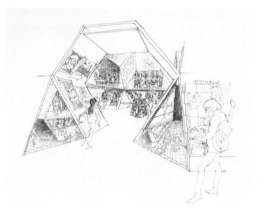

The commission, as well as the controversy, of Safdie's design all resulted from students' initiative. Selected by students who had agreed to help pay for the building, Safdie engaged them in a participatory design process. "A static building would be obsolete before its completion," Safdie noted at the time. "The Student Union must be a place which the students identify as their own, which they participate in building and participate in administering after completion."[10] When the California State College trustees, including Governor Ronald Reagan, rejected his unusual design, primarily on the basis of its incompatibility with the campus's more traditional buildings, students protested with a massive petition drive. Heated debates, student riots, even the resignation of the college's president occurred along the way: "The Union by Safdie will bring fame to San Francisco and to San Francisco State as Safdie's Habitat was universally acclaimed at Expo '67 in Montreal," wrote Reginald H. Biggs, San Francisco State College Advisory Board member in a telegram to the trustees. "But more important, it will bring pride and dignity to the students whose idea it is.... Now, of all times, we need the harmony and enthusiasm which pride and dignity beget."[11] Ultimately, however, the students lost the fight, and Safdie's project was never built.

Model and drawing of walkway leading to bookstore, San Francisco State College Student Union proposal, 1967–68

The final project of the first phase of Safdie's career was his entry in the 1971 competition for Centre du Plateau Beaubourg, today's Centre Pompidou, which was conceived by the French government as a "people's" museum rather than an elite repository of art treasures. Developed in collaboration with his design studio at the Yale School of Art and Architecture, Safdie's entry took second place among the 650 submissions. Like the San Francisco student union, which was conceived as a crossroads of social activity, but larger and on a metropolitan scale, the competition entry was a daring concept that housed museums, restaurants, theaters, and a library connected to a regional train station. Its sunken plaza opened to the surrounding historic streets and was surmounted by a cantilevered museum and library building with a rooftop garden. Adapting Habitat's scheme of flexible and expandable modules to more public contexts, both the San Francisco State College Student Union and the Centre Pompidou competition entry manifested a new kind of urbanism that would accommodate exponential growth, rapid change, and a mobile population.

Model, Centre Pompidou competition entry, Paris, 1971

Exterior (above) and interior,
Yeshiva Porat Yosef, Jerusalem,
1971–91

While launching his career as a professional architect, Safdie also published his first two books, setting the pattern of developing writings as bridges between the various phases of his career, not only helping him to clarify new directions in his work, but also to articulate his evolving attitude toward architecture and its role in society. Taken together, these books — *Beyond Habitat* (1970) and *For Everyone a Garden* (1974) — summarized the successes and failures of Habitat and its progeny. At the same time, *For Everyone a Garden* anticipated the next phase of Safdie's career in Jerusalem. In a final chapter entitled "Meeting Places," Safdie stressed that successful meeting places, from interior atria to outdoor plazas, need to be conceived holistically — from their siting; to the scale of their architectural elements; to the patterns of movement, pedestrian or otherwise, through them. While Safdie cited historic Georgian urban ensembles, as well as his unbuilt projects in San Francisco and Paris, as exemplars, he also described two of his current projects in Jerusalem — the Yeshiva Porat Yosef and the Western Wall Precinct proposal — that were embedded within the ancient city, concluding with questions that would characterize the next phase of his career: "Can one create a contemporary vernacular and reestablish the basic values of the environment? Can one build continuity from the old to the new?"[12]

THE FUTURE OF THE PAST

The second phase of Safdie's career coincided with his establishment of a branch office in 1970 in Jerusalem, to which he still commutes from the United States for about one week per month. Safdie's work during this period combined his interests in social activism and advanced technologies with profound respect for historic and regional context. Over the next six years, Safdie laid the foundation for a new aesthetic of progressive contextualism — a way of thinking globally about building. Here, too, was the genesis of his contemporary global practice.

With the outbreak of the Six Day War in the spring of 1967, Safdie, who was still living in Montreal, sought to enlist in the Israeli military, but the conflict ended before he could leave Canada. He did, however, return to Jerusalem where he finished Israel's compulsory military service and opened an office. His timing was serendipitous. Victory had returned Jerusalem's Old City to Israel, which created opportunities for significant architectural projects. Safdie renovated housing in the Block 38 district (1972–83), where he still keeps an apartment, and the Hosh Complex (1976–78) in styles sympathetic to the area's historic arched and domed architecture.

The dense fabric of the Old City had a profound and lasting effect on Safdie as a visionary urban thinker. Safdie's 1982 book, *Form & Purpose*, summarized the lessons learned from ancient cities like Jerusalem. "City squares," he noted in the book, "are the living rooms of the city, and the conception of each individual structure involves the manner in which it joins others to form the rooms of the city.... It is difficult to think of indigenous architecture in terms of individual buildings — often a line can't even be drawn between one building and the next."[13] Safdie focused on the Isfahan bazaar, "an institution," he wrote, "that makes its demands on the design of every adjoining structure. It functions as a connector so that the mosque, the school, the bathhouse, and the whole hierarchy and network of public spaces — linear or contained, covered or open — can be plugged in."[14] This interest in historical town-making would resonate in the "urban living rooms" he would later create in cities around the world.

Two of Safdie's architecturally significant projects in or near the Old City from the 1970s are religious in nature: the Yeshiva Porat Yosef (1971–91) and the Hebrew Union College (1976–98). At the yeshiva, a residential college for students training to be rabbis, Safdie moved beyond Habitat's rectangular module to a more complex geometry based on spheres. A pyramid-shaped complex of stucco domes, half-domes, and quarter-domes rises above massive masonry walls pierced by stairways connecting the city's Jewish Quarter with the Western Wall plaza. The domes create spatially complex interiors enhanced by the use of prismatic skylights. At the Hebrew Union College — a 300-student facility with classrooms, a library, a museum, and a youth hostel — Safdie showed a strong debt to Louis I. Kahn, for whom he worked in the early 1960s, in his sophisticated blending of traditional and modern materials and forms. Rough-cut, golden-colored Jerusalem limestone clads the complex's exterior walls, creating a fortresslike edifice that relates to the adjacent Old City in both form and material. Inside, the complex becomes more open. Individual building pavilions surround garden courtyards. Trellised and arcaded walkways are built on two separate levels: one for religious students, one for non-students. Limestone here takes a background role, contrasting with reinforced structural concrete, glass, and brushed stainless steel.

Jerusalem's return to Israeli hands in 1967 also led to Safdie's most significant urban design proposal for the city. After the Six Day War, Israel demolished the old buildings in front of the Western Wall, Judaism's holiest site, access to which had been denied to Israeli Jews since 1948. Seeking to make the space an even grander "meeting place," not unlike his Paris competition entry, Safdie proposed excavating the entire site. Never undertaken, his design comprised a series of stepped terraces that would lead to the wall and descend thirty feet to the original street created at the time of Herod, the great master builder before the birth of Christ who had expanded the Second Temple to legendary scale and grandeur.

During this period Safdie also began the recently completed Mamilla Center, a twenty-eight-acre commercial and residential development that is an extension of the Old City of Jerusalem. Here Safdie has sought to link not only old and new, but also east and west, Arab and Jew in both its urban planning and its imagery. Today it completes a vast quarter that also includes a highly controversial Safdie-designed hotel and a residential complex named David's Village. Describing Safdie's early work at Mamilla, Esther Zandberg, architecture critic of the influential *Ha'aretz* newspaper, bemoaned the destruction of an old neighborhood as well as the area's unabashedly commercial character and what she considers the ersatz nature of Safdie's progressive contextualism, which she termed "the Jerusalem syndrome." "The quest for 'local identity,'" Zandberg continued, quoting the catalogue from an exhibition at the Tel Aviv University gallery, "the surrender to the 'physical and spiritual dimensions of the city,' and the attempt 'to strike roots in the earth'…all gyrate wildly in the Mamilla project. The abundance of local means of expression — arches, curved roofs, stone facing and stepped building (which has somehow become a local argot even though Jerusalem's natives never used stepped building techniques) make the walls of the Old City on the other side of the new fast road seem like a faded, inconsequential afterthought."[15] Facing this criticism, Safdie proved himself a flexible and pragmatic architect who could go beyond style (the final, commercial component of Mamilla totally eschewed "the Jerusalem syndrome"), while he remained adamant in his defense of his design on the grounds of its successful urbanism, the opportunities it offers "for meeting, for shopping, for tying in to other things," and his utopian vision of uniting the city's diverse populations.[16] Zandberg, however, remained unconvinced. "I don't think architecture can make the connection between the two nations. It is so naïve. Maybe it belongs to some 1960s belief," she said of a credo Safdie holds dear, "that architecture can make a better world."[17]

From a national and symbolic perspective, Safdie's most significant work in Israel is at Yad Vashem, the fifty-acre site in western Jerusalem that was established in 1953 as the nation's memorial to the Holocaust. In contrast to the Berlin memorial designed by Peter Eisenman — a completely abstract composition of almost 3,000 unmarked stone slabs at street level with a subterranean information center — Safdie's three projects at Yad Vashem — two memorials and a history museum conceived and built between 1976 and 2005 — have moved from literal memorialization toward a fusion of abstract form and representational content that expresses the story of the Holocaust in narrative

Following Spread
Drawing of Yeshiva Porat Yosef, dated February 10, 1986

חי עולם   אי תעות

הלב"

מעת ספדית אדריבלים · דח' מפילא 15 · ירושלים

Model of Western Wall Precinct
proposal, Jerusalem, 1971–85

terms. Based on the Jewish tradition of annual lighting of candles to honor the dead, his memorial to
deceased children (1976–87) repeats the image of five candles infinitely via mirrors in a dark, tomb-
like room. His memorial to people transported to concentration camps (1991–94) includes an actual
Polish train car poised at the edge of a broken railroad track cantilevered over a hill, literally on the brink
between life and death.

Safdie's most recent project at Yad Vashem, a history museum completed in 2005, is one of his
most powerful works to date: "This building may be the most moral statement made by architecture in
our time," Martin Peretz wrote in *The New Republic*, representing the majority opinion. "Its rendering of
the life of the murdered is searing and subtle."[18] The museum, a 650-foot-long triangular concrete tunnel, slices through one of the site's hills. Inside, the tunnel, dimly lit by a thin skylight at its apex, descends
and narrows, and visitors walk on a circuitous path in near darkness, learning about the rise of the Nazis
and the Holocaust in intensely personal ways made possible by extensive research into victims' lives. As
visitors leave the museum, the tunnel's walls open out onto a panoramic view of a sunlit Israel, founded
in the Holocaust's wake. "I had the notion of taking you into the mountain," Safdie has said of his intentions, "with sloping floors and spaces that are more like archeology than architecture. Then, after the
exhibition on the death camps, you see the light at the end of the tunnel, and the floor begins to rise
again — then you come out and see the landscape, and there is a sense of renewal and hope."[19] "I had to
fight for this," Safdie told the *Wall Street Journal* about the building's final uplifting message. "Not everyone on the Yad Vashem board thought this optimistic gesture was the right thing to do."[20] Nor did every
critic — to Esther Zandberg the building offered up "an embarrassing simplicity of symbolism."[21]

While Safdie's work in Israel has been primarily in Jerusalem, he has also worked on a number of
projects in Tel Aviv. There, his ultramodern design for the Ben Gurion International Airport (1995–2004),
which serves the entire country, demonstrates the nation's forward-looking aspirations. Its glass-
enclosed, scissor-shaped ramps dramatize the ideal of open borders, as arriving and departing visitors

cross each others' paths. The airport's shopping arcade, visible to incoming travelers through a glass wall, features an inverted dome pierced by an oculus through which rainwater flows — a metaphor, some have noted, for the Israelis' capacity to make the desert bloom.

TRIUMPH OF AN OUTCAST: NORTH AMERICA

While Safdie's career flourished in Israel in the 1970s, it wasn't until the early 1980s that building commissions emerged first in Canada and then the United States, inaugurating the third phase of his career. Coincident with opening a second, and now primary, office in Boston, this phase was marked by significant building projects across North America. Often powerful expressions of civic and national identities, many of these structures featured grand, populist gestures, most notably skylit lobbies and increasingly dramatic forms.

At the time, Safdie shared many of his colleagues' disenchantment with modernism — its anti-urbanism and lack of richness and complexity — but he never turned to the neo-classical columns and moldings adopted by architects such as Charles Moore and Robert Venturi as antidotes to modernism's sterility. Safdie lacerated their efforts as ironic and arcane pastiches that only other architects would understand in his controversial article, "Private Jokes in Public Places," published in the *Atlantic Monthly* in 1981. This issue would become a matter of public debate in just a few years when Safdie's unbuilt proposal for twin towers at New York's Columbus Circle met stiff opposition from New York journalists, preservationists, and prominent citizens, not only for its height and bulk, but also for its modern style. While *Boston Globe* critic Robert Campbell praised the design as "an astonishment.... Even for Manhattan, this is a building of enormous gusto and chutzpah," *New York Times* architecture critic Paul Goldberger advocated a concept based on the Depression-era Rockefeller Center.[22] Safdie instead continued to build on the traditions of twentieth-century modernism, situating himself alongside contemporary architects Renzo Piano and Norman Foster. "We grew out of modernism," Safdie recently told the *Wall Street Journal*, "and we evolved it further. We made it more contextual. We expanded its technological base. And we started dealing with the sensual and symbolic aspects that modernism tended to avoid."[23]

That Safdie could expand modernism in just these ways was expertly demonstrated in his design for the National Gallery of Canada in Ottawa. In 1983 Safdie won the competition for the country's first purpose-built national gallery of art, vying against such leading Canadian architects as Arthur Erickson and Barton Myers.[24] Completed in 1988, the National Gallery was a pivotal project in Safdie's career. Representing the "Triumph of an Outcast" (considered such because decades had elapsed between Habitat and his next Canadian commission, according to a 1988 cover story on Safdie in *Maclean's* magazine), the National Gallery was the most significant of the architect's many Canadian projects that have come to define the country's national identity. "As if Canadians could never quite persuade themselves that their art was worthy of a building of its own," John F. Burns wrote in the *New York Times*, "governments here procrastinated for more than a century before heeding the urgings of the National Gallery of Canada for a permanent home.... Tomorrow, the long wait will end."[25] "Here was something new in the world," Anthony Lewis concurred, "dazzling — and Canadian. Its architect, its materials, its links to history: all Canadian."[26] In its design, the building featured some of the architect's first great communal spaces — a monumental stairway, a glazed colonnade overlooking the museum's commanding site, and an elaborately skylit great hall — that characterize his current work, juxtaposing the grandiosity of a great civic room with intimate spaces for viewing art. An ingenious system of chimneylike wells with skylights that bring daylight into ground-floor galleries demonstrated Safdie's mastery of natural light, a skill that would be employed to great effect in future projects. Building on the lessons he learned in

National Gallery of Canada, Ottawa, Ontario, 1983–88, with Notre-Dame Cathedral beyond

Canadian postage stamps with Moshe Safdie and National Gallery of Canada

Following Spread
Sectional drawing of National Gallery of Canada by Moshe Safdie, dated August 6, 1983

Model of Crystal Bridges Museum of American Art, Bentonville, Arkansas, 2005–11

Jerusalem, Safdie's National Gallery also sought to work within its historic context: the conical shape of the museum's great hall, for example, evokes the buttressed roof of the nearby Library of Parliament.

The National Gallery of Canada is only one of many Safdie projects to advance an ancient tradition of pedestrian-oriented urbanism in North America's automobile-centered culture. In this phase he successfully created lively civic arenas such as the Salt Lake City Public Library and the Peabody Essex Museum (1996–2003) in Salem, Massachusetts, where he united two halves of the city by connecting them with a serpentine central atrium. Safdie's place-making abilities have also been applied to less dense, traditionally urban sites. Situated along the heavily trafficked 405 Freeway in Los Angeles, the Skirball Cultural Center was Safdie's first American project. Working closely with the institution's planners, Safdie not only designed the new complex, but also helped shape its mission to increase visitors' understanding of the Jewish experience and American life, while offering a rich program of art and culture to the Los Angeles community.

Part college campus, part small town, the Skirball is a series of separate pavilions and landscaped outdoor rooms that arc along the freeway's curving path and take full advantage of the Southern California climate and the site's mountainous terrain. The complex is located on two levels built into the hillside and connected by external stairways. Unlike the way visitors experience the Salt Lake City Public Library, where transparency simultaneously offers multiple views, at the Skirball patrons primarily savor the complex sequentially, encountering a range of rich and sometimes surprising architectural features. Unified by a palette of concrete and pinkish granite, the Skirball comprises pavilions housing vaulted and pitched-roof galleries with skylights letting in filtered rays of the region's celebrated golden sunlight; a glass-enclosed, semicircular auditorium; a café opening onto an outdoor courtyard; ancient archeological fragments; shaded arcades; and landscaped ravines. All help create an intimate sense of urbanism within the largely undifferentiated expanse of greater Los Angeles.

The success of the Skirball's campuslike setting of pavilions attracted the attention of Alice Walton, who commissioned Safdie to design the new Crystal Bridges Museum of American Art in Bentonville, Arkansas. A series of pavilions with concrete-and-glass walls and structural laminated-wood beams is arranged around shallow reflecting pools created by damming a nearby stream. Gently set within a public park, the result is a seamless integration of art, architecture, and landscape that promises to offer the region a new gathering place.

Safdie's ongoing interest in geometry as a generator of architectural shape took new directions in this phase with his embrace of the computer, which offered the means to create new and dynamic forms. Located at the intersection of two rivers near downtown Wichita, Kansas, Exploration Place Science Center (1994–2000) was a seminal project in the evolution of Safdie's form-making. The building's volumes, containing exhibition galleries and theaters devoted to science, were determined by the intersection of its undulating walls and the surfaces of two huge "toroids" or "tori," i.e. surfaces of revolutions formed by turning a circle in three-dimensional space. (Doughnuts and inner tubes are examples of tori.) The center's monumental geometries give formal cohesion to the center's various components and its new public park, while providing the city with a visually dramatic civic signature.

Safdie has also continued to use metaphoric imagery to move projects beyond the purely programmatic, touching, he has noted, "on the most subtle issues of character and symbol as expressed by architecture." In the United States Institute of Peace Headquarters, which was commissioned in 2001 for a prominent site adjacent to the Lincoln Memorial in Washington, DC, the computer-generated, spherical geometry of the steel-frame and white, translucent-glass roof suggest the wings of a dove, the symbol of peace. Safdie had used a similar aesthetic and metaphor at the Yitzhak Rabin Center for Israel Studies in Tel Aviv (1997–2010), a complex comprising a museum, library, and research institute

Model view (left) and rendering of waterfront event plaza (top) and grand arcade (bottom), Marina Bay Sands, Singapore, 2006–10

honoring the assassinated Israeli leader. Situated on an escarpment on top of an abandoned wartime emergency-power generating station, the former station, according to Safdie, "gave me the metaphor for Rabin the warrior," while the free-form, resin-and-fiberglass roof, which seems to float, "represents the breakout of Rabin as peacemaker."[27]

In addition to Safdie's architectural prowess, his projects' successes have also derived from understanding his clients' aspirations. A documentary film chronicling the four-year process of developing the Salt Lake City Public Library from architect selection to opening day made it clear that Safdie was selected for his ability to listen to and engage with the project's diverse constituency, from library and government officials to an especially active public. Moshe Safdie, library director Nancy Tessman noted, made the client "a full player" in designing the building. Another commentator remarked that the library was nothing less than "the physical manifestation of its egalitarian design process."[28]

GLOBAL CITIZENS

Entering a new phase of work at the end of the twentieth century, today Moshe Safdie has a global architectural practice, working in the world's most dynamic emerging markets from India to China, Singapore, and Dubai. Characterized by their greater geographic range, these projects are also on the whole being realized in shorter time spans and are larger in scale than projects of previous phases. Designing megascaled projects on virgin sites for governments with global ambitions has propelled Safdie to move beyond the progressive contextualism he used in ancient Jerusalem and historic Ottawa. Topping the list is the commission for the $5 billion, forty-acre Marina Bay Sands resort in Singapore that Safdie won in a competition with the Las Vegas Sands Corporation. (Safdie had met its board chairman, Sheldon Adelson, at the opening of the Yad Vashem history museum, prompting Safdie to tell the *Wall Street Journal* how "strange" client/architect connections are in today's global marketplace.[29]) Located on a site across the bay from downtown Singapore, the complex will integrate a waterfront promenade, multilevel retail and civic spaces, and an ArtScience Museum shaped like an upwardly stretched hand with

Khalsa Heritage Centre, Anandpur
Sahib, Punjab, India, 1998–2011

finger-like, skylit galleries. Anchoring the complex will be three fifty-story hotel towers surmounted by a cantilevered two-acre "sky garden," a privatized version of the landscaped roofs Safdie used in his earlier projects like the San Francisco State College Student Union and the Salt Lake City Public Library.

Safdie's newfound global reach can be seen in two other recent proposals: the 1.3-million-square-foot Guangdong Science Center (2002–2003), Safdie's competition entry for Guangzhou, China, and the proposed Palm Jumeirah Gateway Mosque (2008) in Dubai. Like Wichita's Exploration Place, both sit on prominent waterfront sites that serve as civic gateways and use bold, curving geometric forms to create iconic images. For the Guangdong Science Center, just as he did in Exploration Place (though far bigger in scale in the China project), Safdie exploded the project's program—an international conference center and exhibition galleries—into three pavilions of swooping shapes. Guangdong also continued Safdie's use of metaphoric imagery—the galleries' forms were inspired by scientific phenomena such as double helixes and molecules—while the Gateway Mosque underscored his expert control of natural illumination. "The praying hall is about a sense of uplifting and light," Safdie has written about the interior where shafts of light from perimeter skylights are reflected off the space's spherical inner surface, forming ever-changing geometric patterns. "Though the mosque is windowless," Safdie has written, "there is always within it a powerful sense of the surrounding universe, our planet set within the constellation in dynamic motion of the solar system. In the words of the Koran: 'Allah is the Light of the heavens and earth.'"[30]

Yet another strange architect/client intersection earned Safdie the commission to design the Khalsa Heritage Centre (1998–2011), now nearing completion in the Punjab section of India. This commission came to Safdie when the region's chief minister visited his children's memorial at Yad Vashem and was overwhelmed by its emotive force. A major public endeavor—its ground-breaking ceremony was attended by 500,000 people in a celebration that included confetti-showered parades of school children, Sikh warriors, and elephants—the Khalsa Centre celebrates 500 years of Sikh history. Similar to Crystal Bridges in its multi-pavilion planning centered on a series of reflecting pools, the seventy-five-acre Khalsa Centre extends Safdie's progressive contextualism to a new region and a new set of meanings.

Acknowledging the Sikhs' history as celebrated warriors, the buildings' volumes seem to rise from nearby sand cliffs and are clad with sandstone, evoking the fortress cities of Rajasthan, Gwalior, and Punjab. The upwardly curving roofs are covered in stainless steel, which, Safdie notes, "complements the traditional reflective gilded domes of the Sikh temples such as the famous Golden Temple, but downscaled to silver, as befits a secular institution."[31] The interiors of two gallery pavilions are gathered in groups of five, representing the Five Virtues, a central tenet of Sikh faith.

Ever aware of the changing world around him, Safdie has seriously considered the social implications of working globally and creating mega-scaled buildings and complexes—a subject he explored as early as 1997 in his book *The City After the Automobile*, written with Wendy Kohn, and to which he has returned in his recent monograph. "Everywhere in the world we find examples of expanded regional cities," Safdie wrote in the book's first chapter, "cities which in recent decades have burst out of their traditional boundaries, urbanizing and suburbanizing entire regions, and housing close to a third of the world's population."[32] In response to such contemporary problems as urban sprawl and congestion, the book proposed a fictional city called "Urbana" made up of a group of civic centers called "New Cardos," in honor of the spines that ran down the centers of ancient Roman and Greek cities. Urbana would integrate regional planning policies that would lead to more open space; new ideas in transportation—private ownership of automobiles would be replaced by public transportation, and rented cars would be treated as a public utility; and innovative architecture—city arcades would have moving sidewalks under retractable roofs.

Beyond its futuristic aspects, *The City After the Automobile* also extended Safdie's thinking about architecture's social role and confirmed the value he places on optimism and progress. In a chapter entitled "Confronting Mega-Scale," Safdie continued his critique of postmodern design leveled in "Private Jokes in Public Places" and openly criticized the efforts of architects such as Leon Krier, who seek to turn the clock back and create nostalgic visions of "charming pre-industrial villages…which completely ignore contemporary conditions of population, commerce, and transportation."[33] In the book and even more recently in the second volume of his monograph, Safdie took specific aim at the pessimistic resignation advocated by Dutch architect Rem Koolhaas, who, Safdie says, urges the architectural profession to "dare to be utterly uncritical" in the face of "apocalyptic demographics…[and] the seeming failure of the urban."[34] In contrast, Safdie sees hope in the future. Specifically, he feels that infrastructure can be used as a generator of urban design and an effective strategy for dealing with mega-scale. By infrastructure, Safdie means "a constellation of elements: the civil engineering response to site-specific features such as rivers, harbors, terrain; the salient urban features such as the *cardo maximus*, or central artery; the bazaar; the aqueduct; the boulevard; the galleria; the highway; the transportation systems. This interconnection of specific site features and urban constructions has traditionally given order, structure, and scale and provided the lifelines for a city."[35]

From the pedestrian pathways threading their way over the roofs of the San Francisco State College Student Union to the terraced Western Wall Precinct, the crescent-shaped atrium of the Salt Lake City Public Library, and the waterfront promenade of Marina Bay Sands, Safdie's architecture and urban planning have shown a consistent adherence to this infrastructure-based strategy. At the same time, Moshe Safdie's people-oriented designs reaffirm his core belief in bringing together client and architect, citizen and city. "But to decide that we are innocent and helpless bystanders," Safdie has written, "is surely no response worthy of us as a society."[36]

Computer rendering of Palm Jumeirah Gateway Mosque, Dubai, 2008

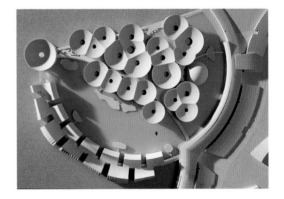

Aerial view of model, Guangdong Science Center, Guangzhou, China, 2002–03

PORTFOLIO

Selected Buildings 1967–2012

This portfolio brings together eleven of Moshe Safdie's most significant projects. Along with the Salt Lake City Public Library, the subject of this catalogue's opening photo essay, these buildings follow the arc of Safdie's career from his seminal Habitat housing complex for Montreal's Expo '67 to projects throughout the world, many of which are still under construction. These commissions also encapsulate the major themes and preoccupations of Safdie's still-vibrant career. They range from his interest in new materials and technologies, including digitally produced forms and spaces, to a synthesis of architecture and landscape; a masterful manipulation of natural illumination; and a capacity to create buildings that, while rooted in local place, represent powerful symbols of culture and ideology.

Habitat

MONTREAL, QUEBEC, 1964–67

Habitat, a highly publicized exhibition pavilion at the 1967 World's Exposition in Montreal, better known as Expo '67, grew out of Moshe Safdie's thesis project at McGill University. It remains a pioneering example of prefabricated housing with the amenities of single-family homes and the densities and lower budgets of urban apartment housing. Habitat is composed of 365 prefabricated concrete boxes, lifted into place by cranes and connected to each other by rods, cables, and welding to form 158 residences. Dwellings range in size from 600-square-foot, one-bedroom units to 1,800-square-foot, four-bedroom units. In total, there are fifteen different floor plans. Offering individual dwelling units and private entries and gardens similar to free-standing houses, Habitat's apartments are accessed from pedestrian skywalks. By overlapping the boxes, the roof of one unit serves as the garden terrace for the one above. All parts of the building, including the units, skywalks, and elevator cores, work together as load-bearing members. Habitat's original plan integrated residential, commercial, and institutional facilities into a single complex, but only a small portion of this original proposal was built.

Hebrew Union College

JERUSALEM, ISRAEL, 1976–98

Located just outside the Old City walls, the Hebrew Union College is a 300-student facility with classrooms, a library, an archeological museum, and a youth hostel. The college characterizes Moshe Safdie's approach to architecture in ancient Jerusalem, where he first developed his aesthetic of progressive contextualism by fusing modern and traditional materials and forms. The exterior walls of the complex, clad in rough, golden-colored Jerusalem limestone, comprise a series of screens, garden walls, and arcades that define the boundary of campus while creating a fortresslike edifice in harmony with the historic surroundings. The campus's interior is spatially more open and contemporary in its material palette. Individual building pavilions surround lushly planted garden courtyards defined by trellised and arcaded walkways on two separate levels: one for religious students, one for non-students. Here, limestone is used more sparingly in favor of reinforced structural concrete, glass, and brushed stainless steel.

National Gallery of Canada
OTTAWA, ONTARIO, 1983–88

Won by Moshe Safdie in a competition, the commission for the first permanent home for the National Gallery of Canada is the most significant of Safdie's projects that have helped to shape Canada's identity. The National Gallery was also seminal in Safdie's own development, presenting some of his earliest signature communal spaces, including a skylit great hall, a grand stairway, and a glazed colonnade overlooking the museum's site on the Ottawa River. Introducing a strategy used on later projects, the building features an innovative system of chimney-like light shafts that manipulates and controls daylight: lined with reflective material, these shafts transmit diffused daylight through the upper-gallery floors to lower-level galleries. Similar to his work in Jerusalem, Safdie's National Gallery takes its cues from its historic and natural context, as is evident in the strong relationship between the conical shape of the museum's great hall and the buttressed roof of the neighboring Library of Parliament.

Skirball Cultural Center
LOS ANGELES, CALIFORNIA, 1986–2012

Located between the 405 Freeway and the Santa Monica Mountains in Los Angeles, Safdie's design for the Skirball Center creates an urban, pedestrian-oriented ensemble within the area's automobile-centric culture. It also responds to the Southern California climate and the site's steep terrain with a series of pavilions linked by outdoor courtyards, arcades, amphitheaters, and landscaped ravines arranged longitudinally along the base of the mountains. The Skirball Center features a museum, changing exhibition galleries, and a conference and educational center, whose focus is Jewish heritage and American democratic ideals. The complex is located on two levels built into the hillside and connected by external stairways. Unified by a palette of concrete and pinkish granite, the Skirball Center's pavilions house vaulted and pitched-roof galleries with skylights that filter natural light; a glass-enclosed, semi-circular auditorium; and a café that opens onto an outdoor courtyard.

Exploration Place
Science Center

WICHITA, KANSAS, 1994–2000

Located at the confluence of two rivers in
Wichita, this project represents a pivotal
event in the evolution of Moshe Safdie's
form-making. The buildings' volumes contain
exhibition galleries and theaters devoted to
scientific and humanistic education. Their
computer-generated forms were created by the
intersection of curving walls and the surfaces
of two huge "toroids" or "tori," i.e. revolutions
formed by rotating a circle in three dimensions.
The form of the "island" exhibition building was
generated by a toroid whose center is high in
the sky, shaping a series of concave roofs facing
skywards like giant receptor dishes. The center
of the "land" visitors' and curatorial building
toroid is deep underground, creating vault-like
roofs descending into the earth. Exploration
Place's monumental geometries visually
unite the center's various components and its
new public park, while providing a distinctive
silhouette on the city's skyline.

Peabody Essex Museum

SALEM, MASSACHUSETTS, 1996–2003

The oldest continuously operating museum in the United States, the Peabody Essex was constructed in several phases over the past 150 years. The objectives of its major expansion and reorganization were to create an architecturally dramatic addition emblematic of the institution's new identity as a museum of art and culture, to unify a disparate group of buildings and join them with expanded gallery space, and to help make the museum a coherent whole welcoming to visitors. In response, Safdie has produced one of his defining urban spaces: a curved, glazed arcade aligned over an existing street forms the spine of the new wing and weaves together the old and new buildings around a courtyard. A series of two-level, house-like galleries, scaled to echo Salem's historic residential fabric, is strung along one side of the arcade. Spaces between these structures allow natural light into both lower and upper levels.

Ben Gurion International Airport

TEL AVIV, ISRAEL, 1995–2004

This new airport serves as Israel's principal gateway and represents the country's most optimistic aspirations. A land-side complex accommodates ticketing, customs, immigration, and baggage claim; an air-side complex includes a glazed connector and rotunda, accommodating food, retail facilities, and passenger services, with concourses radiating outwards to landing gates. Departing passengers check in and descend through the connector into the rotunda and down the concourses to their gates. Arriving passengers ascend through bridges at the gates to a mezzanine level overlooking the concourses and the rotunda, then descend towards passport control through the connector. The glass-enclosed, scissor-shaped ramps dramatize the ideal of open borders, as arriving and departing visitors cross each others' paths, while the connector serves as a ceremonial gateway in both directions. The airport's rotunda features an inverted dome pierced by an oculus through which a waterfall flows.

Yad Vashem Holocaust Museum

JERUSALEM, ISRAEL, 1997–2005

This museum, located within Israel's fifty-acre national memorial to the Holocaust, is a 650-foot-long, triangular concrete tunnel that traverses one of the site's hills. Visitors walk through this dimly lit narrow space, tracing the development of Nazism and the horrors of the Holocaust, based on historical research into victims' lives. The Hall of Names, located at the end of the museum, is a conical structure extending more than thirty feet high that houses the personal records of all the Holocaust's known victims. An underground cone echoes the upper chamber in form and commemorates the unknown. As visitors leave the museum, the tunnel's walls open onto a panoramic view of a sunlit Israel, metaphorically linking the Holocaust to the country's founding. The Yad Vashem site also includes the Yad Vashem Children's and Transport Memorials, also designed by Safdie.

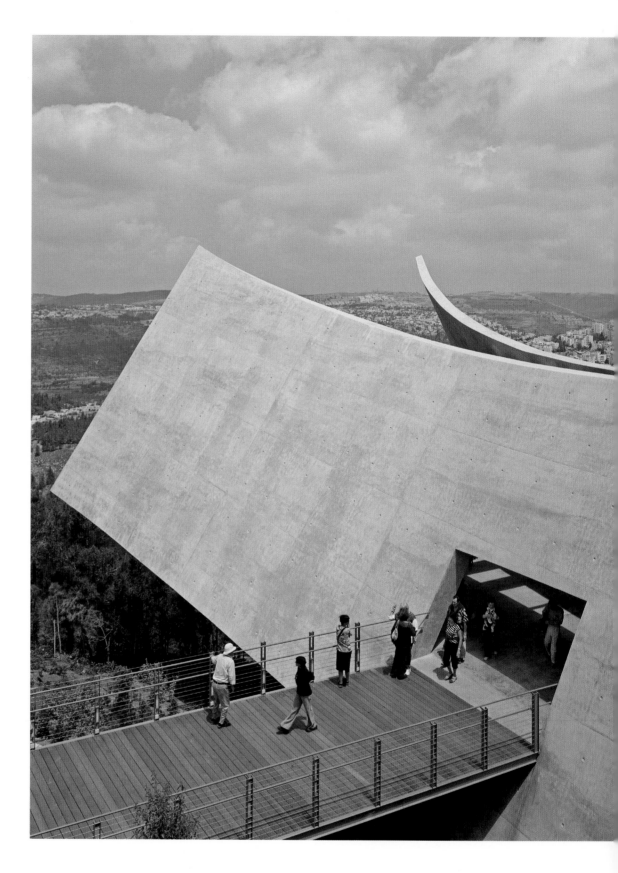

Khalsa Heritage Centre

ANANDPUR SAHIB, PUNJAB, INDIA, 1998–2011

Confirming Moshe Safdie's status as a global architect, the Khalsa Centre demonstrates Safdie's interpretation of progressive contextualism for a new region, integrating cultural and religious symbolism related to the history of the Sikhs. The structures are situated in the holy town of Anandpur Sahib and contain a museum celebrating 500 years of Sikh history and the 300th anniversary of Khalsa, the scriptures written by the founder of the modern Sikh faith, as well as an auditorium, a library, and a memorial. Located on a seventy-acre site overlooking the town, the project includes two complexes that straddle a ravine and are connected by a bridge. Acknowledging the Sikhs' history as celebrated warriors, the building's volumes seem to grow out of nearby sand cliffs and are clad with local, honey-colored sandstone, conjuring up images of ancient fortress cities. The concave roofs are covered in stainless steel, which complements the traditional gilded domes of Sikh temples, but downscaled to a more modest silver befitting a secular institution. The clustering of the galleries in groups of five is based on a core Sikh belief in the Five Virtues.

United States Institute of Peace Headquarters

WASHINGTON, DC, 2001–11

Commissioned in 2001 for a site adjacent to the Lincoln Memorial in Washington, DC, this facility comprises research facilities, a conference center, and a museum dedicated to the theme of peacemaking. The building is organized around two atria—the first serves as the centerpiece for the spaces devoted to scholarly research, while the other is a focus of public activity and conferences. The public spaces in the building are roofed by a series of undulating spherical and toroidal segments whose forms were computer-generated. White during the day and glowing from light within at night, the steel-frame and translucent-glass roofs suggest the wings of a dove, the symbol of peace. Safdie had used a similar geometry and metaphor at the Yitzhak Rabin Center for Israel Studies (1997–2010) in Tel Aviv, a complex comprising a museum, library, and research institute honoring the assassinated Israeli leader.

Crystal Bridges
Museum of American Art

BENTONVILLE, ARKANSAS, 2005–11

This project is Moshe Safdie's most recent achievement of a seamless integration of art, architecture, and landscape. The Museum is composed of pavilions arranged around two ponds created through a weir system which manages the flow of a natural stream through the complex. Two bridge buildings are located at opposite ends of the ponds: the northern bridge contains galleries; the southern bridge contains reception, dining, and hospitality facilities. Other buildings house a multipurpose great hall, galleries, classrooms, a library, curatorial spaces, and administrative offices. Set gently within a natural ravine on 120 acres of Ozark forest, the project's design aims to protect the natural beauty of the site and to emphasize a strong sense of place. The materials are from the region: building walls are architectural concrete with wood inlays, the roof is a system of laminated-wood beams, and glass is used extensively to integrate interior and exterior environments.

ARCHITECTURE AS VOCATION

Sarah Williams Goldhagen

The ethic of conviction and the ethic of responsibility are not absolute opposites. They are complementary to one another, and only in combination do they produce the true human being who is capable of having a "vocation."
— Max Weber

Throughout the history of modernism, architects and critics have determined what constitutes the relevant in contemporary architecture in response to cultural fashions; economic conditions; and political, social, and technological aspirations and realities. Today's polynucleated discourse on architecture and urbanism is no different. Open the newspaper, log on to the Internet, pick up a shelter magazine. What are the topics du jour? Among the most frequently discussed are the possibilities offered by digital technologies to create new forms, new materials, and new modes of construction and fabrication. Then there is the profession's loss of control over matters that traditionally have belonged in its domain, such as the articulation of the program, the oversight of the process of construction, and the design not just of buildings but of larger chunks of our urban environment. Most compelling are the consequences of globalization and global warming on urban settlement patterns, modes of design and building, social relations, and the formation of cultural identity.

Moshe Safdie's work, encompassing different typologies, scales, and practices in the built environment, powerfully grapples with the challenges of building in today's world: the changing role of the architect in the face of the exponential growth of large-scale urban regions; globalization's impact on human settlement patterns, social relations, and cultural identities; the architect's role in shaping not only an individual project's program but its larger civic role; the complex formal innovations made possible by new digital technologies for design, construction, and manufacturing. Responding to the growth of large-scale regional conurbations, Safdie, in his writings and a series of regional plans, urban plans, and master plans for new towns, has proposed various strategies to responsibly manage growth. To stay the homogenizing tides of globalization, he creates pockets of locality in varied contexts. In buildings around the globe, he has taken advantage of new manufacturing processes and new digital technologies to create dramatic, previously unexecutable forms, and then assiduously worked with manufacturing and construction firms to tweak those forms in order to maximize efficiency in their construction.

In light of all this, one might think that Safdie's work would be central to today's architectural discourse, and yet one only infrequently finds mention of it. Why? There is a quick answer: the blast furnace of Safdie's intellect, combined with his deeply committed approach to architecture, has conferred upon him, in his pronouncements and his work, the wisdom and the curse of maintaining a critical distance from the immediate. Safdie approaches design not as the fabrication of photogenic moments, but as a vocation, and he designs from a larger ethical framework that is uncommon in contemporary international practice.

In Safdie's insistence that the architect's design choices must be anchored to a deeply considered philosophy of architecture's actual and possible roles in society, culture, and politics, he swims against the current of contemporary architects who tend towards resigned pragmatism

("I'm an architect, not a politician," Robert A. M. Stern recently quipped after accepting the commission to design the George W. Bush Presidential Library) or the twinned cynicisms of "criticality" (Peter Eisenman and his many minions) or "post-criticality" (Rem Koolhaas and his). Repeatedly, Safdie tells his colleagues, "We have choices." Architects can accede to an unjust and inhumane world or pretend that what they do professionally bears little relevance to such problems. Or architects can instead choose the more difficult path of approaching the design of buildings and cities as a vocation. In that case they must navigate their careers as Safdie does, using as their compass the values of social commitment and responsibility.

But this quick answer, adequate as it may be in our front-running-driven, media-mediated world, conceals a deeper, more profound answer that helps us to understand the nature and distinctiveness of Safdie's contribution. To unearth this answer, we can begin by revisiting two moments in his work. The first is his brilliant, still-fresh prototype for prefabricated, multiple-family urban dwellings, Habitat, which was constructed for the World's Exposition in Montreal in 1967 and which first earned him his global reputation. We shall return to analyze Habitat later. For now, consider the project in light of today's renewed fascination with prefabrication. After Expo '67, Safdie reworked the Habitat model in the hopes, as he writes in *Beyond Habitat* (1970), of enticing local government officials and private developers in New York City, Jerusalem, Tehran, San Juan, and elsewhere to build it. All these campaigns failed, leading him to conclude that neither he nor any architect would be given the opportunity to execute prefabricated social housing on a large scale. Doing so, he had learned, would require multiple unrelated institutions to rethink their priorities and to coordinate their modes of operation, including federal, municipal, and local governments; various branches of private industry; and private citizens who formulate and abide by social norms governing their private and public lives. So Safdie, pragmatically, turned his attentions to more executable aspirations and visions. Since then, architects have concocted a succession of proposals for prefabricated dwellings. These have been met with varying levels of fanfare; most have been subsequently shelved. Dreams of well-designed, inexpensive housing live on, but mass-produced housing has never materialized. For precisely the reasons that a prophetic Safdie reluctantly decided, it likely never will. Safdie was ahead of his time. Instead of riding the horse for all it was worth, he wisely dismounted. Those behind him are still galloping their way to futility.

The second instance pertains to Safdie's more recent work. Even when his projects directly relate to contemporary debates, they flout common practices. When designing, Safdie envisions how he hopes users will experience the building. If that experience demands complex forms—as in, for example, the Peabody Essex Museum in Salem (1996–2003)—then he designs complexity. The roof of the Peabody Essex's multistory public atrium is a single curve in plan and a double curve in section because that is what Safdie decided would help create the sense of processional climax he sought. Yet, unlike many of his colleagues, he has never pretended that "complexity" constitutes some sort of profound intellectual project, nor does he advance the misguided notion that architecture might be sculpture. Moreover, he disciplines even his most complex forms with clear geometries to maximize efficiency in construction and the use of materials. (Not to do so would be to fall prey to "capriciousness," one of Safdie's most damning obloquies.) To complicate the picture further, he is just as likely to employ traditional Euclidean geometry as he is parametric design. If he thinks that his users and publics need legible imagery, he designs it, even as many contemporary designers shirk (or pretend to) overt symbols.

All this points to a dominant feature of Safdie's approach to design: it is rigorously multifaceted and extraordinarily complex. Understanding his projects requires abjuring simple notions of what is hot or new. It requires putting away one's laptop, closing the book on high-resolution photographs, and traveling to sites. It demands the willingness and determination to both look at the project and beyond it, to explore the full scope of practices mastered to bring it to completion. Finally, it necessitates questioning unspoken assumptions and reflexive reactions about style — a rarity in analyses of architecture and urbanism today.

Describing and evaluating Safdie's accomplishments pose daunting challenges that might make even Atlas shrug. From his office come regional plans, airports, skyscrapers, multi-pavilion complexes, courthouses, museums, memorials, public parks, and more. He is the master-of-many-disconnected-trades that the good architect must necessarily be, and yet few are. In his practice and sometimes in a single project, he synthesizes infrastructure, regional, and city planning with urban design, landscape architecture, and architecture. In doing so, he transgresses the boundaries that artificially parse our built environment into disconnected practices. He designs from a wide-angle lens, with the understanding that inserting a building or complex of buildings into a preexisting landscape is, inherently, a socially aggressive act: one literally reconfigures a world.

Over the years Safdie has proposed several master plans for new cities or large-scale developments in existing cities. History has demonstrated that the large scale, immense cost, and political complexity of such projects ensures that most are never executed, as was the case with Safdie's projects for Keur Farah Pahlavi (1975–78) in Senegal, Simpang New Town (1994) in Singapore, and West Kowloon Reclamation (2001) in Hong Kong. But one of Safdie's master plans is now a living city, Modi'in, which promises to reach its target-projected population of 200,000 within years. Modi'in, commissioned in 1988, welcomed its first residents in 1996, and today is a city of 70,000 spreading over a complex terrain of hills and valleys. Sited between Israel's two major urban and economic centers, Jerusalem and Tel Aviv, Modi'in serves as a bedroom community, especially for families with two wage earners who commute in different directions. Safdie, who has always advocated a two-state solution to the Israeli-Arab conflict and refused to build Jewish settlements in the West Bank, which Modi'in abuts, also hopes that the city will become a home for displaced Jewish settlers once a peace agreement is finally reached with the Palestinians.

To build Modi'in, Safdie donned one professional hat after another: urban and land use planner, political activist, infrastructure and transportation specialist, urban designer, landscape architect, and architect. Given the complexity of today's world and its urgent political, environmental, and social problems, contemporary architects must be willing and able — both — to skillfully take on such a wide array of roles. Yet I know of very few contemporary practitioners who are. Safdie, by contrast, does it again and again. For Modi'in, he, along with architects in his Jerusalem office, wrote the city's zoning provisions, planned the transportation infrastructure, developed the land use plan, wrote the design codes, oversaw and wrote the landscaping guidelines for all the city's public parks, and designed the community and retail center. The residential parcels were sold in blocks to developers, who built the bulk of the city's buildings according to their own designs.

Modi'in's plan builds upon a number of widely celebrated postwar urban designs. Indeed, before beginning the project, Safdie's office studied and compiled a research book on new towns built after 1945. Some precedents for Modi'in include Le Corbusier, E. Maxwell Fry, and Jane Drew's Chandigarh (1951–59); Sven Markelius's new town of Vällingby (which opened in 1954); Josep Lluís Sert's plans for Cimbote, Peru, (1948–51) and his Peabody Terrace complex in Cambridge (opened in 1964); and Giancarlo de Carlo's university buildings and town plan in Urbino (which began in 1962 and continued for many years). In Chandigarh, Le Corbusier, Fry, and Drew devised a system of wider thoroughfares connecting neighborhood blocks, with smaller streets running within each larger block. In the new town of Vällingby, the first of a number of new satellite towns outside Stockholm, Markelius rejected the abstract formalism and high densities of earlier modernist precedents. He chose instead to build

Site plan (this page) and
aerial view (opposite page)
of Modi'in, Israel, 1988–ongoing

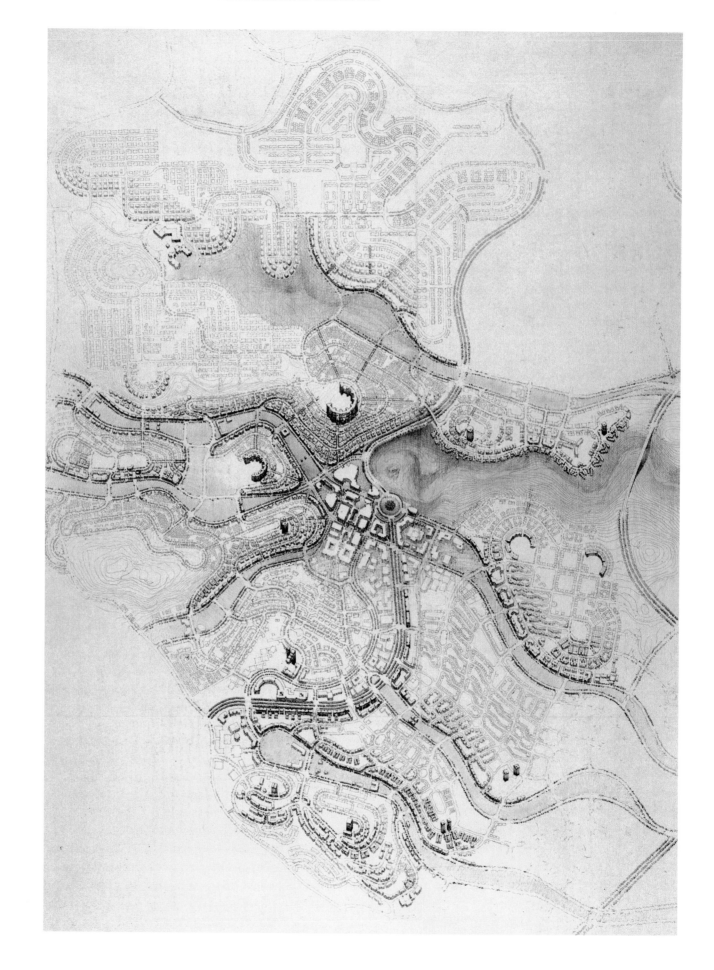

Mamilla, Jerusalem, ca. 1970

The protective wall separating
Mamilla from "no man's land,"
1948–67

a medium-density garden city along the site's preexisting topographic contours, placing public spaces and transportation nodes in the town center, surrounded by a variety of differently configured neighborhoods and residential housing types. Sert's Peabody Terrace is a model of fairly high-density urban housing that also offers a potent sense of locality, created by a visually provocative, contrapuntal composition that articulates different kinds of lawns and urban plazas. The site plan was meant to knit the housing complex into the surrounding community and probably would have done so if its owner, Harvard University, had not consistently undermined or destroyed the social intentions of the original design. Perhaps most relevant to Safdie's master planning and urban designs are Giancarlo de Carlo's urban designs, preservation plans, and Collegio del Colle in Urbino. De Carlo's work in Urbino was widely admired in the 1960s and early 1970s for its sensitivity to historic precedent and the existing contours of a site and its demonstration of how a combination of accommodating existing conditions and good architectural planning can help to nurture strong communal bonds. De Carlo's Collegio complex offers a variety of indoor and outdoor, public and semi-public spaces in the form of patios, arcades, amply proportioned outdoor passageways, and staircases to fortify a sense of communal identification.

Modi'in's master plan builds on, then betters, these celebrated predecessors. It draws from some of their best features, such as site-specificity, constructed hierarchies of public and private spaces, sensitivity to historic precedent, variation of housing types, and density in residential sectors. Those features are knit together within a well-conceived infrastructure: well-designed urban plazas and parks, and a road system that facilitates both efficient movement and neighborhood congregation. At the same time, Modi'in's master plan embodies and extends Safdie's architectural, urban, and social principles. He began with a comprehensive analysis of the site and decided to modify the typical urban settlement strategy of placing the city's principal arterial roadway in the valley where it would be easiest to construct. Instead, he ran a series of coupled boulevards along the sides of each major valley. These larger paired boulevards delineate rectangular bands on which are sited neighborhood parks, the local school, and a small commercial area. Threaded through each large neighborhood block are smaller streets for local traffic.

This road system allowed Safdie to leave a substantial portion of the valley floor as a ribbon of green parkland and playing fields. Two- to four-story housing steps and terraces its way up the slopes, much like a traditional Mediterranean village. The residential buildings in Modi'in increase in height relative to their topographical position, with towers—a pragmatic concession to developers' insistent demands for higher density—crowning the summits of the hills.

Unlike most new towns, but like most cities, Modi'in's neighborhood blocks are visually distinct from one another, presumably because different developers built them. Through various provisions in the city's codes, further visual and spatial complexity was promoted. The neighborhoods contain many different kinds of open spaces: each residential cluster combines terraces, courtyards, patios, walkways, and staircases in varying configurations. These fine-grained urban design features, along with the larger contours of the city's plan, foster the social bonds that allow subcommunities to grow within the large neighborhood blocks.

Modi'in is distinctive in the history of new town planning because it combines a number of features that have long been embraced by urban designers, but only in a grab-bag fashion: site-enhancing specificity, a varied supply of housing types and styles, distinctively designed parks and playgrounds to enhance each neighborhood's sense of identity, abundant green spaces accessible to the entire community. Equally important, Modi'in's plan avoids two problems that defeat many new towns: visual and spatial homogeneity on the one hand, or, conversely, excessive spatial differentiation of one neighborhood unit from another. The former produces boredom; the latter discourages residents from mixing socially, making it difficult for them to develop a common sense of communal identity. Modi'in, in contrast to many other postwar new towns, boasts a lively, urbane sense of community.

The crowning achievement of Safdie's planning and urban design projects is surely his recently completed master plan and urban, architectural, and landscape design for Mamilla in the Hinnom Valley in West Jerusalem, on which he has been working for more than thirty years. As he did in Modi'in, and in order to accomplish what he has in Mamilla, Safdie and his office sustained — over many years, many clients, many vocal opponents and lawsuits, and many changes in government — a determination and commitment to succeed; an unceasing engagement in public life; and a pragmatic willingness to selectively cede to commercial, political, and economic contingencies. As in Modi'in, Safdie and his office also mastered an array of planning and design challenges, including land use law, zoning codes, transportation planning, historic preservation, large-scale construction on a historically and politically charged territory, urban design, landscape architecture, and architecture.

Stern House in Mamilla Center, Jerusalem, with numbered masonry blocks to facilitate its reconstruction, 2008

The Mamilla quarter runs along Jerusalem's Old City walls from the Damascus to the Jaffa Gates, along a portion of the "green line," the former border between Israel and Jordan. For nineteen years this area created what was literally a no-man's wasteland of barbed wire and garbage that politically divided the city into a poor, Arab section to the east and an economically developing, modernized Jewish section to the west. The protracted, early stages of the Mamilla project, during which Safdie was working for KARTA, a combined federal-municipal organization, produced the master plan that was largely adhered to in the final scheme (except in its provision to put two major roads underground). The plan laid out a residential sector to the south called David's Village, which now also includes the David Citadel Hotel, and a mixed-used commercial and residential center to the north called the Mamilla Center. This stage also entailed clearing existing slums, resettling its residents (all Jewish), re-parceling the land, rewriting zoning codes, and analyzing and developing an infrastructure and transportation plan. This iteration of the master plan called for the preservation of only one building, the nineteenth-century French Hospice of Saint Vincent de Paul. Later, Safdie's office conducted studies of the site's historic buildings in order to select a wider range of buildings meriting preservation and developed a variety of preservation strategies — restoration, renovation, adaptive reuse — tailored to each building's condition and historic value.

Mamilla Center, looking toward the Old City, 1972–2009

The mixed-use Mamilla Center, which runs along the Old City's walls and terminates at the Jaffa Gate, is the jewel of the project. This carefully considered, deeply impressive urban design towers above recent comparable projects such as Renzo Piano's cramped master plan, homogenized buildings, and sorry public spaces in the Potsdamer Platz in Berlin. The Mamilla Center materially refutes those many critics of planning and of modernism, as well as contemporary practitioners, who maintain that it is impossible to execute such a large-scale project in a socially responsible manner. Packed into this more-or-less triangular, twenty-eight-acre sloping site is a large, nearly invisible parking garage for cars and tourist buses, and rising above it are a hotel, a luxury condominium cluster, several office buildings, and an amply proportioned pedestrian promenade that begins at a busy downtown intersection and terminates at the Old City's Jaffa Gate.

One of Safdie's favorite urban types is the Cardo in ancient Roman cities, the colonnaded commercial and transportation main street lined with shops displaying their merchandise. The Mamilla Center's promenade offers a contemporary reinterpretation of the Roman Cardo, along with changing views of two of the Old City's most prominent monuments, David's Tower and the Citadel of David. Contemporary buildings, designed by Safdie, are woven through historic ones. These include the French Hospice and the nineteenth-century Stern House, where Theodor Herzl once slept and which Safdie's office had dismantled block by masonry block, warehousing its numbered stones for years while infrastructure construction proceeded, then reconstructing it on its original site when construction on the complex

Mamilla Center arcade

neared completion. For the newly constructed elements of the promenade, Safdie wisely opted for a vocabulary of highly abstracted historicism, deferring to the language and materials of existing buildings and taking advantage of their human scale without aping them in their details. Old is old and new is new. Threaded between these historic buildings is an arcaded promenade containing retail shops, cafés, and restaurants. Above is the occasional pedestrian bridge linking the multistory buildings on either side.

The arcade, which in some places covers nearly half the twenty-four-foot-wide walkway and is extended with half-arc trellises on which vines will eventually grow, offers protection from the summer's blazing sun and the winter's chilling rain. As one approaches the entrance to the historic, walled Old City, commerce falls away. "Why should a private developer do anything to limit independent control over a large investment?" Safdie asks, writing about the Mamilla Center in *The City After the Automobile* (1997). "Because as a society, we acknowledge that private developers are now constructing our public domain. And therefore, they should be subject to public-minded planning and zoning." Near the Jaffa Gate the promenade becomes a purely public space: a landscaped, multilevel outdoor plaza.

Taken as a whole, the Mamilla Center replaces a former no-man's slum land with a lively, historically resonant, thoroughly contemporary, mixed-use commercial and retail district laced with different kinds and sizes of vibrant, appealing public spaces. It weaves together a fistful of this politically charged, polycentric, multiethnic city's frayed edges into a successful public space where, on most days, one sees religious and secular Jews, Arabs, Armenians, Christians, and tourists mingling and interacting. The pedestrian promenade, a rare example of architecture triumphing over political adversity, will surely take its place among modernity's most beloved public spaces, such as the Galleria in Milan and Rockefeller Center in New York City.

The admixture of architectural and social vision, professional versatility and public-mindedness, that drove the Modi'in and Mamilla projects to their successful completion has also generated some of Safdie's most remarkable buildings. Here we shall select examples from just two typologies: dispersed-pavilion complexes such as the Hebrew Union College in Jerusalem (1976–98); the Skirball Cultural Center in Los Angeles (1986–2012); the recently opened Khalsa Heritage Centre in Anandpur Sahib, Punjab, India (1998–2011); and the Crystal Bridges Museum of American Art in Bentonville, Arkansas (2005–2011); and continuous-periphery, aggregate-volume civic projects such as the Peabody Essex Museum (1996–2003) and the Salt Lake City Public Library (1999–2003). The character of these projects, like Modi'in and Mamilla, is built up from sensitivity to climate, natural topography, and the historic fabric of the site. They are not just figural objects but holistic, particularized places. They are also designed with a sensitivity to human scale; the determination to make lively, vibrant public spaces; and an understanding of design strategies that promotes such uses. In these projects some more strictly architectural aspects of Safdie's vision are also manifested. Interior spaces receive natural light even when sectional innovation is required, clearly articulated circulation patterns offer a variety of spatial and visual experiences, and structural systems and geometric forms underlie the projects' formal expression.

Beginning with the Hebrew Union College, Safdie has, in larger cultural and educational institutions, often chosen to disperse programmatic elements into compositionally distinct-but-linked pavilions. These are not only among Safdie's best buildings but are also among the best sole-authored building complexes in contemporary architecture. Multiple semi-freestanding pavilions are arrayed along their sloping sites, interspersed with landscape elements (often planted with indigenous plants), paved patios, and outdoor plazas. Linking the pavilions and outdoor spaces in carefully managed processional sequence are bridges, indoor corridors, and outdoor walkways.

Each of these projects is simultaneously unique and elaborates on its predecessors. Over the years the geometries controlling the site plans have become looser and more varied in response to topography and the construction of visual and processional axes. For the Hebrew Union College, Safdie broke the program into three rectangular volumes skewed off axis from one another in response to Jerusalem's hilly topography, but he then unified the composition by employing the tartan grid plan. The Skirball Center, next in chronological sequence, also employs the tartan grid to knit together interior pavilions and exterior patios and gardens, but the building volumes themselves are more varied, combining squares, rectangles, arcs, and semicircles. The plan for the much larger Khalsa Centre, which spreads over dozens of acres, deploys arcs, cylinders, circles, and rectangles, along with less conventional geometric figures. The pavilions of the Crystal Bridges complex, located in a woodland and spanning the large Crystal Spring, take their formal arrangement largely from their functions, a series of dams and bridges that do double-duty as one of the most significant museums of American art in the United States.

Khalsa Heritage Centre,
Anandpur Sahib, Punjab, India,
1998–2011

Safdie's approach in all of these projects has been to break what would otherwise be extremely, perhaps even excessively, large buildings down to a more human scale and simultaneously allow nature a designing hand. In *The City After the Automobile*, writing of what he calls "mega-scale," he exhorts his colleagues to challenge clients' insistent demands for enormous buildings: "We must critically evaluate the assumptions that lead to super-scaled places…we should be asking [clients], how many people require being in the same building?" In these projects nature and architecture interpenetrate, highlighting the particularistic qualities of the place, helping to orchestrate complex circulation patterns and imparting a lively sense of urbanism. Even in the most rural of settings, as is the case with Crystal Bridges, users take in views of other pavilions, other gardens and plazas, and other people.

To emphasize how these projects promote their users' sense of the particular qualities of a place, it is worth examining at least one in more depth. The commission for a museum and heritage memorial to the Sikh religion came about because the Punjab's Chief Minister, Parkash Singh Badal, wanted to mark the 300th anniversary of the Khalsa, the scriptures written by Guru Gobind Singh, with a building celebrating 500 years of Sikh history. It may come as a surprise to learn that Sikhs and Jews share a number of religious convictions and cultural experiences. According to Safdie, he earned the commission for the Khalsa Centre because Badal, on a visit to Israel, was so impressed with the recently completed Yad Vashem Holocaust Museum (1997–2005) in Jerusalem that he called Safdie, spoke of the affinities between the two religions, and offered him the commission. Sikhism, like Judaism, is a monotheistic religion. Many of its canonical codes of conduct implicitly reject the basic beliefs and practices of Hinduism, Islam, and Christianity. Sikhs believe that all people—not just Sikhs, not just Brahmins, not just those who have accepted Allah or Jesus—are equal before the eyes of God. Like Jews, they are prohibited from worshipping idols or proselytizing, and they are obligated to give generously to charity and to respect other religions in word and deed. Also like Jews, Sikhs have suffered centuries of religious and political persecution.

Jaisalmer Fort, Rajasthan, India

Anandpur Sahib, a city of over 13,000 in the Punjab province, is one of Sikhism's four holiest sites and an annual pilgrimage destination for hundreds of thousands of believers. According to Sikh legend, it was in this city that Guru Gobind Singh performed the first Amrit ceremony, whereby Sahajdharis are baptized, symbolizing their lifelong commitment to abide by Sikhism's strict codes of conduct. (Once baptized, Sahajdhari Sikhs become Khalsa.) Safdie had spent time in northern India, working on Louis Kahn's Indian Institute of Management in Ahmedabad. Like Kahn and scores of other modern architects, Safdie was taken with the area's architectural monuments: the asymmetrically balanced site plan of Fatepuhr Sikhri; the fusing of landscape, architecture, and memorial in Mughal mausoleum gardens; the strange, abstract forms of the Jantar Mantar in Jaipur; and imposing, cliffed fortress-cities such as Jaisalmer. Safdie, accepting Badal's offer, traveled to Anandpur Sahib, where he discovered that the government authorities' chosen site was many kilometers outside of town. Such an important memorial and museum

Peabody Essex Museum, Salem,
Massachusetts, 1996–2003:
site and elevation sketch by Moshe
Safdie (top), site plan (middle), and
completed building in context
(bottom)

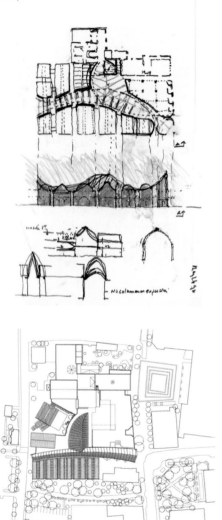

must be accessible by foot, especially to the many pilgrims who visit the city each year. He suggested a more centrally located site, spanning a ravine and close to Kesgarh Sahib, the seventeenth-century fortress marking the location where the tenth Khalsa performed his legendary baptismal ceremony—and the authorities agreed.

A comparison of how Safdie manages topography and natural light in the Skirball Center and the Khalsa Centre encapsulates his sensitivity to his buildings' sites. Where natural light falls in the Skirball Center, the Khalsa Centre is flooded with shade. The Skirball Center's architectural vocabulary extends the late modernism of Kahn's nearby Salk Center in La Jolla; the Khalsa Centre's sheer, monumental, shadowy volumes recall both Kahn's Indian Institute of Management and the fortified Jaisalmer. The L-shaped western part of the Khalsa Centre, closest to town, contains a library, temporary exhibition spaces, and a restaurant, with its inner edge articulating an outdoor entrance plaza abutted by a 400-seat auditorium. Western and eastern parts of the complex are linked by a 24-by-450-foot-long, Roman-arched bridge straddling the ravine. The memorial and the permanent exhibition galleries are housed within the large, multileveled, amphitheater-like arc, which contains both indoor and outdoor circulation spaces. The arc visually culminates in a concatenated cluster, as imposing as a man-made cliff, of five cylindrical and rectangular prisms symbolizing the five virtues of the Sikh faith.

A number of Safdie's smaller buildings on urban sites, such as the Salt Lake City Public Library and the Peabody Essex Museum, read from their exteriors as single blocks but are actually comprised of multiple volumes prised apart in one or several places. Designed and planned with careful attention to climate and surrounding buildings, streets, and pedestrian pathways, the Salt Lake City Public Library and Peabody Essex Museum buildings—both located in cool, northern climates with long winters—combine human-scaled interiors with multistory public atriums drenched in natural light. Both buildings serve as fulcrums in their urban settings and bring together diverse populations and microcommunities, much like Modi'in's many parks and the Mamilla Center's pedestrian promenade.

The public library in Salt Lake City was one of the most heavily used in the country even before the completion of Safdie's new building in 2003, but since then use has tripled. Salt Lake City, which has a population of approximately 181,000, looks like many western American cities. Set on a grid, wide, multilaned roads function as spatial barriers dislocating one enormous city block from the next. Along these roads stand mainly undistinguished one- or two-story buildings, occasionally fronted by an asphalt stretch of parking. Rising from several downtown blocks are high-rise office towers. In such dispersed, auto-centric urban circumstances, very few public spaces are to be found, and anything one might call a public is less in evidence still.

Salt Lake City's most distinctive feature is not architectural but natural: the monumental, reddish-ochre Wasatch Mountain Range outside the city. However, across from the new library, on Main Street, is the imposing Salt Lake City and County Building (1894), a four-story, gray, Richardsonian monolith topped by a 256-foot-high clock tower, standing alone on its ten-acre block of a site in a large expanse of lawn. To the new library's west, on a wide, busy boulevard, runs the light rail line that terminates on the campus of the University of Utah.

Although approximately 62% of Utah's residents belong to The Church of Jesus Christ of Latter Day Saints, fewer than 50% of Salt Lake City's residents are Mormon, and the city has a large Hispanic population (over 19%), as well as substantial student and gay communities. When the city outgrew its old library, the library's director, Nancy Tessman, began to develop both an architectural program and a larger vision for the new building. She wanted the Salt Lake City Public Library to be a social condenser, a destination point that would not only welcome but would regularly bring together the city's diverse and overlapping communities. In short, Tessman wanted the Salt Lake City Public Library to create a public realm in a city that really had none. Cannily, Tessman decided that not just the building itself but the process of building it could jump-start her project in community creation. She developed an unusually rigorous selection process in which a short list of four architects was asked to develop preliminary proposals. Then, in a series of widely publicized meetings, they presented their proposals and received feedback from city authorities (who would be appropriating funds for the project), library staff members (who would work in the building), and the public.

In the end the selection was not difficult. According to Tessman, Safdie proved to be the only architect who did not "talk down" to his many audiences. He was as receptive to feedback from laypeople and library staff as he was to those who would formally be his client. He listened with an open mind, thought on his feet, and proposed viable alternative solutions on the spot. Safdie also demonstrated a respect for the specificity of the site that was unmatched by the other contenders. For the facade of the new library, he told Tessman that he wanted the focal point to be not his own building but the imposing Salt Lake City and County Building, which is listed on the National Register of Historic Places. "Right now," he said, referring to the building, "it's lonely."

The design of the five-story Salt Lake City Public Library squares the relentless geometric grid of the city with the sensuous irregularity of the surrounding mountains in plan and elevation. The plan is deceptively simple: a triangle (housing the main library) is lined on one of its three sides by a rectangular block (containing offices for the library staff), on another by a two-ply, arcing, ochre concrete wall (containing, inside, retail spaces at ground level and reading rooms above, and outside, a generously proportioned staircase). Inside the building that same arcing wall encloses the glazed, multistory public atrium. Outside, it articulates a public plaza and amphitheater and steps down to offer bleacherlike seating on which people can sit and lunch in good weather and which they can ascend to get elevated views of the city.

The rectilinear office block presents a sedate, almost deferential facade, echoing in overall volume and proportions the previously "lonely" City and County Building across the street. One enters the building at the street corner, where the building's rectangular, triangular, and arcing volumes meet, into the eighty-foot-high public concourse. Here the composition becomes looser, more distinctive, and more monumental. The rectilinear facade appears to peel away from the body of the building as it launches into its curve toward the mountains and the outdoor public plaza behind. The light-drenched atrium, open to the public at all times, is activated by a glass-enclosed elevator, a series of small retail shops, a café with seating, and views into the lower level where the facilities and rental rooms are located.

To enter the library proper, one crosses bridges spanning the lower level. With this gesture Safdie deftly solves two problems: he gets natural light to fall into even the building's lowest, below-grade level, and he finesses one of the principal challenges of library design, which is to provide a single access point so that library staff can monitor the comings and goings of their users to ensure that goings are only for the library's users and not its unchecked books. The bulk of the library is contained within the triangle of the plan. These interior spaces are quite low-ceilinged—after all, this is a project that was completed for approximately $200 per square foot—but Safdie ensures that they are never oppressive through two design elements. The triangular prism of the library is quite shallow, and two of its three external walls are faced with floor-to-ceiling glass, so that natural light and glimpses outside—toward the mountains or toward the atrium—are never far away. Furthermore, shallow barrel vaults visually interrupt the sweep of the library's long-spanned interiors. Necessary for structural reasons, these barrel vaults also create the visual and phenomenological impression that the library is comprised of human-scaled pockets of space rather than one continuous spatial plane.

Salt Lake City Public Library,
Salt Lake City, Utah, 1999–2003

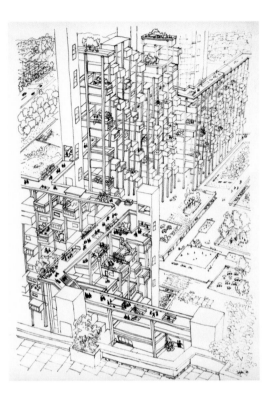

Drawing by Moshe Safdie
of "A Three-Dimensional
Modular Building System," his
undergraduate thesis project,
McGill University, 1961

In the Salt Lake City Public Library, Safdie eschews the sort of overt symbolic gestures that he often employs and which sometimes rankle his detractors. The skylit, glazed, multistory area between the library proper and the office block, a concatenation of steel, glazing, tension wires, and pedestrian bridges, shows the abstraction of modernism at its best. Such a moment suggests that we might circle back to reconsider Safdie's use of symbolism in his other projects. In the Peabody Essex Museum, for example, overt symbolism is employed in its vernacularizing brick volumes, which echo the building's immediate surroundings, and in its curving, hull-like ceiling structure, which recalls the ships that made Salem the capital of eighteenth-century marine trade. In light of how often Safdie achieves a delicate balance of nature, structure, metaphor, and abstraction; in light of his indisputably valuable, deeply considered social agenda for architecture; in light of how frequently he manages to successfully manifest that agenda in his designs, perhaps it is time for critics to reevaluate their aversion to Safdie's overtly symbolic motifs. Is the discourse on architecture really so paltry as to let one aspect of Safdie's style — the most photographable aspect, to be sure — determine how his formidable contributions to architecture and the social world will be assessed?

The context of these more recent projects helps cast his much smaller, widely celebrated Habitat '67 in a new light: it was an anomaly that, in its successes and its failures, pointed the way to Safdie's future. Habitat is a residential complex in an oeuvre of mostly civic projects, the product of a search, now largely abandoned, to find a solution to the problem of low-cost, prefabricated social housing. The concerns driving Habitat's design have shaped many of Safdie's most consequential subsequent projects. From the standpoint of urbanism, Habitat stood by the city and against urban sprawl and proposed that only medium-to-high-density housing would create humane urban centers. Modi'in and Mamilla advance more sophisticated versions of the same proposition — and so do most of Safdie's urban-minded contemporaries. Fusing architecture and landscape architecture, Habitat offered "for everyone a garden." All the projects discussed here, from Modi'in to the Salt Lake City Public Library, insist upon the same. In plan and section, Habitat develops a hierarchy of public, semi-private, and private spaces, a theme that is greatly elaborated upon in the other projects discussed here. In design concept the piled-up prisms of Habitat offer every unit different views and kinds of natural light. Through the design codes for Modi'in, and in the spaces of the Khalsa Heritage Centre, the Crystal Bridges Museum of American Art, and the Salt Lake City Public Library, Safdie constructs a sophisticated variety of sequences, views, and types of natural light. In style, Habitat's Lego-like evocations of vernacular, multifamily dwellings — Taos Pueblo, Mediterranean coastal towns — are both historically resonant and abstract. That is a theme that courses through many of Safdie's subsequent projects in ways that vary from each to each.

To analyze Safdie's work in this sequence, from the largest in scale to the smallest, from the most recent to the earliest, is not simply some fancy parlor trick. It makes a point. Safdie has always begun his designs with the understanding that his is a vocation that "affects the lives of billions." His projects currently under construction, such as the Crystal Bridges Museum and, more significantly, the mega-scale Marina Bay Sands mixed-use complex in Singapore, are designed from within the same ethical framework and with the same social aspirations. Each project is both of the world and has the potential to become, as Kahn once put it, a world within a world. From an impressively early age, Safdie has had an idea of what he wants that larger world to look like. His own projects, large and small — his worlds — have both developed out of and evolved that vision.

■ ■ ■ ■

Revisiting four moments in Safdie's biography offers a more fine-grained understanding of his complex, holistic architectural vision and further clarifies how the projects discussed here relate to that vision. Simultaneously, it sheds light on Safdie's outside-in/inside-out role in contemporary architectural discourse. The accretion of his early experiences—his childhood in Haifa, his architectural training at McGill University in Montreal, his short employment with Kahn, and his tenure as director of the department of urban design at Harvard University's Graduate School of Design—lay the foundations for many of his central design tenets. These include a nexus of core beliefs: that making buildings and cities is a social and political act; that the humanistic, contemporary city must combine high-density residential development with vital, provocative public spaces; that architecture must offer resonant public symbols; and that buildings must express their structural dynamics and be efficiently constructed. Encompassing all these concerns is Safdie's central conviction that to responsibly design the built environment one cannot parse it into disconnected or competing practices. One must be city planner, urban designer, landscape designer, architect, and more.

HAIFA

As is well known, Safdie spent his childhood, until he was fifteen years old, in Haifa, a Mediterranean coastal town in what was then Palestine and is now Israel. One could make any number of observations and speculations about the impact of these experiences on his architectural vision. Here we shall emphasize only two sets of salient factors. The first is more strictly architectural. During the years Safdie spent there, Haifa was what Safdie describes as a coastal, pedestrian "Bauhaus hill town." Downtown had an Arab bazaar and a major city street, then called King's Way, which was a large-scale, arcaded street typical of colonial architecture. Spreading up the hills from downtown were Bauhaus-style buildings: the city of Safdie's youth was built up from legible geometries, rectilinear volumes, curved balconies, rooftop terraces, and patios. "It was all steps up and down," Safdie remembers, "with fingers of nature interlaced with fingers of urbanism," just like Modi'in's urban spaces and his pavilion-complex buildings. As in most warm climates, much of daily life was lived outside the confines of the home, in semi-public patios and public plazas, streets, and beaches. This environment nurtured Safdie's convictions, borne out in Habitat '67 and numerous subsequent projects, that architectural forms could support a progressive social agenda, that cities must grow from the contours of nature, and that they should contain concentrations of high-density, residential housing and should offer different kinds of semi-public and public spaces.

The second pertinent feature of Safdie's youth relates to his conception of the architect's vocation. The land in which Safdie was raised was then, and continues to be, one of the most highly politicized societies in the world. Most Jewish settlers to Palestine were, like the young Safdie himself, "ardent Zionists" who believed they were creating for Jews a haven from political persecution and social ostracism. Spirited debate and outright conflict about the legitimacy, and the ideal form, of their society were common, both among Jews and between Jews and non-Jews. Safdie still remembers his anger (partly for political reasons) when his parents decided to leave Israel for Montreal, believing that their departure betrayed Zionism. (Today he holds citizenship in the United States, Israel, and Canada; is married to an Israeli; and runs a branch office in Jerusalem.) From early on, Safdie understood that people's daily lives are profoundly and in every way affected by the decisions people make—or are prohibited from making—including about how to govern themselves and organize their social lives. From this comes his repeated insistence that people—architects—have choices about how to shape their world. To deny this is to turn one's back on the obvious. Worse, it is to set oneself up for a life lived in moral indifference.

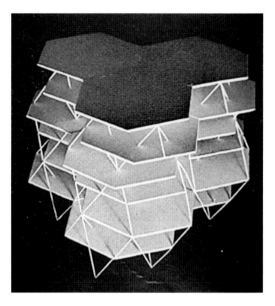

Model of City Tower scheme by Louis I. Kahn, 1952–53

Model of San Francisco State College Student Union proposal, 1967–68

Sketch and plan of Children's
Orphanage, Amsterdam,
by Aldo van Eyck, 1955–60

TEAM 10

Until he was exposed to it during his studies at McGill University in Montreal, Safdie has often said that he never before considered architecture as a profession. Afterwards, he never considered doing anything else. One instructor influenced him particularly—H. P. Daniel ("Sandy") van Ginkel, an émigré from the Netherlands who later became chief planner of Expo '67 and hired Safdie to head the design of the Expo's master plan, for which Safdie eventually built Habitat. Van Ginkel was a founding member of the loosely organized, international group of young architects, Team 10, which was spearheaded by van Ginkel's onetime architectural collaborator, Aldo van Eyck, with whom he had designed a small school in northern Holland, and by Alison and Peter Smithson, a wife-and-husband team from London. Self-anointed Young Turks, van Eyck, van Ginkel, and the Smithsons, along with, among others, Jaap Bakema, Giancarlo de Carlo, Georges Candilis, and Shadrach Woods, coalesced into a group around 1953 and 1954. (De Carlo joined in 1959 after the dissolution of Congrès Internationaux d'Architecture Moderne, or CIAM.) The group became known as Team 10 because they were chosen as a team to organize CIAM's tenth conference, which eventually took place in Otterlo, Holland, in 1959.

The centrality of Team 10 to Safdie's intellectual formation has not been sufficiently appreciated or explored. His refusal to differentiate between architecture and urbanism, his determination to create constructed hierarchies of public and private spaces, his deliberate attempts to emphasize the particularity of place, and his understanding of the centrality of cultural identity in architectural design—principles which Safdie learned from growing up in Haifa—were all canonical tenets of Team 10. The group's foundational document, the Doorn Manifesto (published in 1954 and named after the city in which it was formulated), announced dwelling—which it also called "habitat"—as the challenge of postwar modernism. Safdie's thesis project, which became the starting point for Habitat, was published in 1962 in Dutch *Forum*, the journal edited by van Eyck from 1959 to 1963 and the de facto house organ for Team 10.

Team 10's substitution of the words "dwelling" and "habitat" for CIAM's more commonly used term "housing" formed part of Team 10's larger accusation that the CIAM establishment had neglected the social dimension of modern life. "It is useless to consider the house," declared the Doorn Manifesto, "except as part of a community owing to the interaction of these on each other." The architects who joined Team 10, different as they were, all kept their eyes trained on what they called patterns of human habitation, by which they meant the whole network of social relations in which any individual or family unit is embedded. Like Safdie, they believed that low-cost, well-designed social housing would succeed only if architects took into account that people and families were embedded in and sustained by polycentric, overlapping, and ever-fluid social groups. Team 10 conceptualized these groups in terms of urban space: the street, the neighborhood, the communal gathering space, the city, and the region. Structured hierarchies of human association—from private, to various configurations of semi-public, to public—undergirded the healthy society. Attending to one form of human association, such as the home, without considering its interdependence on others constituted a recipe for failure and irrelevance.

Most members of Team 10 also, as a consequence, refused to differentiate between architecture and urban design, insisting that one can only design individual buildings to both accommodate and express the particular communities they served. Influenced by the emerging discipline of cultural anthropology, these architects believed that buildings must accommodate and make manifest their cultural specificity. No style should aspire to be—indeed, no style could be—"international." The architect's task was to serve a specific client in a specific community by examining local particularistic patterns of social interaction, along with the immediate built environment and the topography and climate of the site. Two projects, both of which Safdie admired, embodied Team 10's deep commitment to cultural specificity: Aldo van Eyck's Children's Orphanage in Amsterdam (1955–60) and Georges Candilis and Shadrach Woods's many published studies for low-cost housing in Morocco under the name of their firm, ATBAT-Afrique.

Safdie admired van Eyck's celebrated orphanage, known to him since his student days at McGill, in which simple geometries were built up into an extraordinarily intricate plan that van Eyck had developed around the concept of facilitating a variety of levels and types of social engagement. In the orphanage van Eyck balanced a hierarchy of spaces to accommodate different age groups of children. In each age cluster, bedrooms were adjacent to a semi-private congregation space containing an outdoor area for play and an indoor one for play, meetings, and meals. All clusters were arranged along a generously proportioned, stepping spine, thus avoiding the anonymity of overly long corridors. Larger outdoor spaces and an indoor auditorium offered places of congregation for the entire community.

As important for Safdie as van Eyck's orphanage were ATBAT-Afrique's various housing prototypes, which they called "habitats," for poor residents of Casablanca's *bidonvilles*. Candilis, Woods, and their partners conducted what they believed to be social-anthropological research into the culture, social mores, and living patterns of their projects' anticipated inhabitants. In their many proposals for low-cost housing, they also tried to accommodate their designs to the hot desert climate of northern Africa, offering proposals on how to maximize natural ventilation and manage sun and shade.

At McGill, van Ginkel imbued his students with Team 10's canonical tenets: that architecture and urbanism were one, that architecture could not be designed without a larger social vision, that buildings and urban spaces must foster many different forms of social interaction in many different kinds of public spaces, that modernism was inconsistent neither with cultural nor with site specificity. Such ideas resonated profoundly with the politicized, highly idealistic young Safdie, who recently had been unwillingly displaced from Haifa, a tightly knit, densely populated city of politically aware, ethnically identified immigrants, to Montreal, a wealthy, spatially dispersed city constructed on the colonial architectural heritage of France and England. Safdie knew that dwellings are much more than just houses. He knew that architecture and urbanism are one. And as the global citizen he became, he understood the inescapability of cultural difference.

TECTONICS AND SYMBOLISM

While still in Israel, before Safdie decided to become an architect, he had planned to study agronomy to prepare himself to create a new kibbutz with some friends. In his backyard he raised bees and was fascinated by the hives bees make: beautifully constructed objects of exquisite structural efficiency, controlled by the order of geometric form. Later at McGill, Safdie studied with Peter Collins, a trained architect and committed proponent of modernism who was especially interested in the technological and material innovations underlying the new architecture. Collins argued that the forms of the new architecture must not only abide by the laws of physics, but also materially express them. Collins's ideas about the structural foundations of the new architecture dovetailed with Safdie's respect for the laws of nature. The synthesis of structure and geometry into efficient form became Safdie's conceptual foundation for architectural design.

The structure and geometry of organic forms captured the imaginations of many young architects in the 1950s and 1960s, including those of the Smithsons and Kahn, whom Safdie approached in 1962 looking for work. Following the lead of Kahn, Anne Griswold Tyng, and others, Safdie steeped himself in the writings of the early twentieth-century biologist D'Arcy Thompson and the postwar cultural theorist Lancelot Law Whyte, who posited that geometry was a kind of secret key to understanding human civilization, a link between the forms of nature and the forms of culture. From this body of thought Safdie developed a number of convictions: that architecture's structural forms must not violate the physical principles of nature, that those principles should be made evident in the final design, that architectural structure must be disciplined with geometric form, and that architectural forms are intrinsically symbolic. In a recent essay Safdie asserts: "The nautilus shell, the bone structure of a vulture's wings, the spider's web are constant reminders that the formally complex is a response to fitness. There is very little capricious complexity in nature's designs!" Architecture symbolizes and is of the cosmos.

Safdie's early explorations into modular or cellular design, evident in Habitat and other early projects, emerged from van Eyck's use of the geometric module in his orphanage and from the ideas of Kahn, Tyng, and others. Although in the end Safdie, like Kahn, discovered that organically derived modularity is too limiting to accommodate all the competing demands that go into the making of architecture, he maintained and continues to hold that tectonic articulation and structural efficiency are the hallmarks of responsible design. He embraces these tectonic principles as ethical imperatives on the same level of importance as the other dimensions of his practice, even in the large-scale, complex buildings that employ multiple structural systems.

MAKING ARCHITECTURE URBAN DESIGN

In 1978 Safdie joined Harvard University's Graduate School of Design (GSD) as professor and director of the program in Urban Design. Josep Lluís Sert, one of CIAM's leaders, had established the urban design program because he believed that in the United States city planners, whose professional roots were not in design but in urban policy and the social sciences, were usurping architects' professional engagement in urbanism. Sert, like Safdie, believed that the architect's vocation by definition included active engagement in public life: while teaching at the GSD, Sert also served as architectural advisor to Nathan Pusey, Harvard's president, and as chair of the Cambridge City Planning Commission. Sert shared with Safdie and many other architects a dislike for the dispersed, suburban settlement patterns then dominating American urban growth. The goals of his GSD program in urban design were to develop a curriculum that would encourage architects, landscape architects, and urban designers to actively collaborate, to engage in public life, to fortify urban centers by increasing the density of residential development, and to create vital urban public spaces such as parks, piazzas, and active pedestrian zones.

For five years while at the GSD, Safdie offered studios on the city of Jerusalem, involving students and faculty from three departments, as well as faculty from other parts of the university. A more electrifying project for young students would be difficult to imagine. Israelis had only recently recaptured East Jerusalem from Jordan in 1967 in the Six Day War, unifying a city that had been split down the middle and inhabited since 1948 by mutually hostile populations, with Arabs controlling East Jerusalem and the whole of the ancient, fortified Old City, and Jews the western portion of the city. The "green line" running right through downtown Jerusalem, a no-man's land, divided the city into Arab and Jewish halves. When East Jerusalem was recaptured, the Israeli government commissioned a new master plan to knit the city together while respecting its citizens' cultural differences. Infrastructure needed to be modernized, zoning laws written, and the area where the green line had run re-urbanized. Each studio grappled with questions of local and national public policy, as well as how to respectfully accommodate cultural differences; plan for current and anticipate future infrastructure needs; assess the value of Jerusalem's historic fabric; decide upon preservation strategies and select which ones should be employed where; use the hilly topography of the city to the best advantage; and integrate architecture, urban design, and landscape architecture into a plan to create vital public spaces that would welcome the city's diverse populations.

At the end of the project, Safdie published *The Harvard-Jerusalem Studio*, presenting five years of accumulated research and a wide array of proposals for master plans and urban designs for selected areas of the city. *The Harvard-Jerusalem Studio* is a masterpiece of architectural, urban, and historical research and of architectural pedagogy. Indeed, it should be required reading for every student of the urban environment. In his Jerusalem studio projects Safdie both extended and deepened the multifaceted, socially committed approach to architecture and urbanism that he had been developing from his experiences in Haifa, at McGill, and under the tutelage of Kahn.

■ ■ ■ ■

Examining these aspects of Safdie's origins helps us to understand the seriousness of his purpose and vision, as well as how he continues to develop and build upon it. It is this, not the vagaries of style or the journalistic moment, that needs to be at the core of any reassessment of his work. We are now in a better position to address Safdie's insider-outsider position in contemporary architectural discourse. The roster of his projects and the high quality of his best ones establish Safdie as one of our most successful serious architects, on par with Renzo Piano, Richard Rogers, Norman Foster, or Frank Gehry. His accomplishments tower above celebrated corporate architects like David Childs of Skidmore, Owings & Merrill or Harry Cobb of Pei Cobb Freed & Partners. His clients and the users of his buildings verge on the unstoppable in the praise they heap upon his work. His projects tend to come in on, or close to, budget. Only rarely do they suffer problems owing to poor construction or design. Among his contemporaries, Safdie alone has single-handedly designed and overseen the construction of what is now a thriving new city: his design for the Mamilla Center in Jerusalem is far superior to comparable urban design projects by other architects.

He has developed a clear-sighted and intellectually powerful analysis of the very real problems threatening our twenty-first-century cities. Among them are the erasure of a sense of locality, the uncontrolled or badly controlled growth of regional conurbations and megalopolises, the multiple ways in which our cities and buildings contribute to global warming, and the atomization of human relations owing to developing technologies of communication and ever-more-rigid class stratification. Through his architecture and urbanism he attempts to ameliorate them—and sometimes succeeds. In an era of heightening social dispersal, Safdie insists upon the importance of vital, uplifting public spaces that attract users of many different classes, ethnicities, and cultures, and he builds them. Unlike many of his contemporaries, Safdie approaches architecture and urbanism not as the practice of making precious jewelry for high-end cultural institutions and fashion designers, but as a social act that governs and changes lives. This demands a multifaceted approach encompassing historical understanding, pragmatism, active involvement in and understanding of public affairs, the willingness to immerse oneself in the nature and culture of a place, and the ability to plan and design not just buildings but urban spaces, landscapes, and cities. In his best projects Safdie puts into practice the social-architectural-ethical objectives that he has developed over many years and repeatedly stated in his many eloquent published writings. To a sometimes disturbingly self-blinkered profession, Safdie's work poses a powerful, discomfiting challenge and, indeed, an ennobling and much-needed model.

See "Notes" for bibliographic sources.

HABITAT OF THE FUTURE

Moshe Safdie

Since its inauguration in 1967, Habitat has witnessed the lives of three generations, suffered forty-three Montreal winters, and endured the passing of several currents of architectural thought—Utopian optimism, into which it was born, followed by postmodernism, deconstructivism, critical regionalism, and the list goes on. Habitat was conceived in hand-drawings and models, engineered by hand-computations and the slide rule, before computers and computer-aided design. It was created to fit into an industry proud of its assembly-line, mass-production techniques, self-sufficient in producing each and every one of its components.

Today, industry has been transformed into globalized, decentralized productions, where a product is made with a great number of specialized components manufactured across the globe. Habitat came to a planet populated with 3.5 billion human beings; now the total exceeds 6.7 billion. Having reached a respectable age, it has weathered well, developed a patina, wrinkles and all. But, above all, Habitat was and is a happy and satisfying home for the 158 families who reside in it.

To revisit the concept of Habitat almost half a century later demands that we reconsider and rearticulate the objectives of this enterprise. What did Habitat aim to provide? How has it lived up to its promise? How might it be improved as a living environment or made more affordable? Or made more sustainable? Or made more adaptable to current urban conditions? These questions draw on issues of lifestyle, social interaction, construction technologies, and real estate economies, to mention but a few of the relevant issues.

Habitat was, above all, about the theme "for everyone a garden," a metaphor for making an apartment in a high-rise structure into what connotes "house"—a dwelling with its own identity, openness in a variety of orientations, and adjacent personal garden space set within a community. One of the charms of Habitat was that it maintained the feeling of an agglomeration of houses, not of high-rise apartment living. The individual identity of the house is maintained—its autonomy within the whole, its abutting garden open to the sky, its multiple orientations transcending the decades-old malaise associated with apartment living.

These qualities were achieved by "fractalizing" the mass of the building. Of course, in 1967 the term "fractal" did not yet exist. (Benoît Mandelbrot was to introduce his new branch of mathematics in 1975.) Yet, essentially, this natural phenomenon—the breaking down into clusters and sub-clusters into what appears to be random, yet is a mathematically ordered pattern—that is the foundation of Habitat's concept. The payoff is that, by increasing the surfaces of the building, we not only multiply opportunities to maximize light and views, but also to transform the mass of large buildings, perforating the surface so that, basketlike, you can see the sky beyond and allow the air to flow through the building mass.

In Habitat this is facilitated by the modular construction. The prefinished concrete module becomes the basic building block, combined to form larger clusters, and even larger assemblies, within the whole. The building block also combines to form a diversity of apartment types and sizes. While fractalizing the mass of the building opens up many environmental opportunities, in it lies the economic challenge. The multiplicity of surfaces is susceptible to energy loss: the building acts as a radiator, demanding extensive insulation, waterproofing, and surface treatment.

Forty-three years of habitation have demonstrated, almost overwhelmingly, the satisfaction of the residents of Habitat in the life provided by its houses. They come to live there and stay there decade after decade because it is unlike either the suburban house they might have lived in or the downtown apartment they might have left. They come and they stay because it seems to have fulfilled the notion that a house can be created within a high-rise, urban structure. They feel that way even though in the winter they must traverse the open-sky street to their apartment and otherwise sustain a life in the harsh snowy climate of Montreal. "For everyone a garden" has also met the challenge of the seasonal cycle, as residents added solariums extending outdoor life to all seasons.

But, with Habitat's success, there have also come the doubters: if Habitat is so wonderful, how come it has not proliferated everywhere? If it provides a superior environment, why do traditional and typical apartment buildings prevail? The answer is, in part, building and real estate economics. As I wrote in 1974, the cost of Habitating is to sustain the greater amenities it provides, recognizing that it will always be more costly both to build and operate than the closely stacked massing of the traditional apartment building.[1] In the vertically stacked apartment building, structural forces will flow directly to the ground, plumbing lines will not be interrupted, and the exterior envelope will be reduced. Habitat's "fractalization," which includes the inclined and stepping massing, plays havoc with the building systems, profoundly affecting the economics of building.

These economic constraints do not apply to or affect the one percent of super-luxury dwellings currently being constructed around the globe, in New York or Dubai, Singapore or Shanghai, Hong Kong or São Paolo. Eminent architects have joined with developers to provide the super-luxury buildings, some stacked traditionally, some dramatically suspended in space, costing many millions of dollars per unit. Indeed, for that market, Habitat today presents an ideal model, as demonstrated by recent projects by Santiago Calatrava and other architects who have joined the developers' quest for this segment of the market. Clearly, however, unless Habitat can respond to the wider demand of middle- and upper-middle-income urban dwellers, it will not proliferate.

HABITAT RECONSIDERED

In deciding to embark on Habitat of the Future, we face the question: how might we do this today at the beginning of the twenty-first century? We must carefully define our objectives if we are to avoid an ambiguous drift, seesawing between questions of economics and density on one hand, and amenity and livability on the other.

Should the study concentrate on maintaining the level of amenity and quality of life provided by Habitat, but in arrangements and construction methods that might crack the economic barrier? Or should one seek to improve on what had been achieved in 1967 as a living environment? In seeking affordability, should one accept, not with an air of defeat, but of experience and wisdom, the necessity of somewhat reducing these amenities, making buildings more compact, reducing the building envelope, and improving the efficiency of the structure? And how does all this sit with the ever-increasing intensity and densification occurring in the mega-cities of the world?

A criticism leveled at Habitat was that, with all the fuss surrounding it, it really wasn't very high density. If it is to meet the needs of Shanghai, Singapore, Manhattan, and Hong Kong, it must respond to the scarcity of land and the ever-increasing pressure for greater densities and mixed uses as it attempts to address the needs of contemporary urbanism and the vast network of closely packed, very high residential complexes and office buildings covering many miles of our megalopolises.

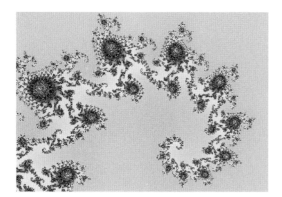

Diagram of fractals by
Benoît Mandelbrot

REGIONAL ADAPTATION

It has been correctly observed that Habitat was conceived with the memory of Mediterranean hill towns, echoing a milder, gentler climate. Reevaluating Habitat today demands that we address the fact that, like the great variation in plant life one would anticipate finding in the northern reaches of Canada as contrasted with the equator jungle, habitation should vary greatly from one climatic region to another. Universal solutions transported from one region to the other (buildings with vast glass areas in a Nordic climate deployed in the ovenlike climates of the Middle East, for example) will not do! What is good for Vancouver is definitely not good for Dubai. The whole notion of light, the changing seasons, the angle and path of sun travel, the penetration of sunlight through the course of the day and the season, and the resulting necessity of insulation and shade for heating or cooling, all vary greatly, not to mention lifestyle and cultural differences.

This is an exciting notion, as it presents the possibility that regional differences will evolve an architecture particular to place, such as the mud-brick structures of the Iranian desert and the braced-wood-and-plaster structures of northern Europe, more greatly differentiating one global city from the other. Wood, brick, stone, thatched roofs, and tiled roofs are each elements of a regional vernacular architecture. With industrialization and the global character of contemporary construction, the constraints now become different. Thus, one anticipates that massing, the relative compactness or openness, the type of building enclosure, the type of outdoor spaces provided, and the nature of public circulation, all become more specific, creating greater differentiation between one applied concept and another.

INDIVIDUATION OF THE DWELLING

In Habitat the prefabricated box was prefinished like a car on an assembly line, with its sophisticatedly designed industrialized bathrooms, kitchens, and windows. Forty-three years of occupancy have proven that people need to, and desire to, reshape their dwelling in their own image. Habitat dwellers have acquired and expanded into adjacent units, burrowed through the concrete walls to connect them, replanned them, added solariums to some of the terraces, reshaped and replanned the number and size of rooms, and redecorated. Today Habitat boasts a full range of unit designs from palatial Louis XIV-like, to slick modern, to Spanish colonial.

The reality, I conclude, is that it is futile to design the dwellings down to the last detail, installing each and every appliance and component, floor finishes, etc. No matter how tasteful the standard unit design, it will differ from the desires and tastes of the residents. You might satisfy some, but you will not satisfy the long line of residents who will follow in years to come.

One of Habitat's great technical inventions was the subfloor, a two-foot-deep space under the floor that provided for air-conditioning equipment and ducts, plumbing, and electrical routing. It was conceived almost in innocence, a method by which we could insulate the cantilevering floors, distribute ducts and plumbing, and install the fan coil units. It proved to be the element that really gave long-term flexibility to the building. The subfloor allowed residents to move bathrooms and kitchens to wherever they wished, to rearrange ducts, and to repartition the space. This facility for flexibility evokes the concept of the loft, the tall industrialized space that is converted to housing. You start with a generous space, well-endowed with windows, which you can plan and subdivide at will.

Certainly, the Habitats of the Future need to internalize this lesson. Whether it is twelve, eighteen, twenty-four, or three thousand square feet that a family or individual might be able to afford, flexible space, well-provided with outlets for plumbing and power, open to daylight in two or three directions, and fronting on an outdoor garden space open to the sky, are the ingredients that make for the improved loft, a space in which residents can now custom-design their house for themselves.

Habitat under construction,
Montreal, Quebec, 1964–67

Habitat, as it was built

Drawing of unbuilt original scheme
for Habitat, ca. 1964

HABITAT STUDIES FOR THE 21ST CENTURY

Our studies for a Habitat for today focus on a number of fundamental issues affecting feasibility, livability, and economic parameters that impact any proposal.

Buildability: Recognizing that the cost of housing is affected by structural complexities, as well as complexities of the mechanical and electrical systems, speed of construction, and the cost of enclosing a structure, some of the studies focused on greatly simplifying these elements as compared with Habitat '67. Some studies were premised on maintaining a simple, vertically stacked structure, traditional plumbing shafts, and greater compactness with reduction of skin area for the buildings. As these simplifications occurred, we pushed the envelope to maintain, as much as possible, exposure to light and optimal orientation, garden spaces for all or most apartments, and greater flexibility in interior planning for the residents.

Density and Mixed Use: A criticism leveled at Habitat in 1967 was that it was, in the final analysis, limited to medium-density housing. Even Habitat's unbuilt original scheme, twenty-five- and thirty-stories high, was not as dense as some of the apartment complexes rising today in Hong Kong and Manhattan, Shanghai and São Paulo. Over the past years, we have increasingly become aware of the development of many urban sites in which both housing and offices — work space, living space, and shopping — comprise the development program. This can be seen in development areas abutting or within the central business districts. In New York, for example, it is the program proposed for such major redevelopment sites as the Con Edison site on the East River and the railroad lands on the west side, as well as developments proposed for the Queens and Brooklyn shoreline on the East River. High density and mixed use go well together. Mixed-use development offers us the opportunity to reshuffle the traditional mode of juxtaposing, side-by-side, office buildings and residential buildings. In the traditional development mode, residential and office towers cohabit alongside one another, often with the result that views and daylight are compromised where they are most needed for residential development, which metaphorically and in reality are built in the shadow of office buildings.

The advantage of mixed-use structures is that functions can be reshuffled three-dimensionally. Retail always thrives along the streets at ground level. Offices naturally form the base of the development, where daylight can often be brought into the larger-footprint buildings through atria. Residential development can be stacked above, benefitting from greater height, views, and light. Stacking office and residential buildings vertically also offers the opportunity for developing horizontal pedestrian streets midway in a high-rise neighborhood, for example, at the transition point between offices (below) and residences (above). Community facilities and some service retail are effectively placed along these streets in the sky. Thus, while the average mean density of the office-residential mix is great, that density's detrimental effect on quality of life is reduced.

STRUCTURAL SIMPLIFICATION

We have embarked on schemes that have emerged from the supposition that the greatest way to improve the affordability of Habitat is to stack the units vertically. Thus, both structure and plumbing are not compromised in their simplicity. In these schemes, the building's envelope can vary, be compact or more open, and massing can be modulated depending on the climatic setting.

As we pursue this strategy, we recognize that one of the qualities of the original unbuilt Habitat design was its attempt to provide a constant sun-exposed face to each and every dwelling. In the original Habitat '67 proposal, the rhomboid membranes sloped, stepping down gently, either to the southeast or southwest. In Habitat '67, as realized for Expo '67, this ambition was not sustained. Units facing the city or river were oriented south, sometimes east, west, or north, providing a greater variety and less constancy of orientation. The sensitivity to the direction of exposure varies climatically. In a tropical setting one might prefer north or south exposures. A dominant consideration would be to assure ventilation by prevailing winds. But, as one moves north (or south) from the equator with great seasonal variations, the need for sun in winter and shade in summer becomes more acute. Hence, orientation becomes less an issue for compromise and more a pre-condition for energy efficiency.

Study Number 1
VERTICALLY STACKED HABITAT

The vertically stacked Habitat proposes to construct the entire complex from prefabricated panel systems consisting of floor slabs and bearing walls, forming continuous, uninterrupted, vertical support walls for the building. While the walls stack vertically to form columnlike supports for the cross-spanning slabs, they also have the capacity to cantilever inwards and outwards in two directions by twenty-six feet. To maintain efficiency of the structure, the full depth of one floor forms the cantilevering beam, minimizing the structural impact.

The result is a structure that is modulated "in and out." It extends outbound towards the east, then recedes to extend towards the west, and so it goes, to the full height of the building. Each dwelling is approximately the same depth, stacking in and out to form gardens for each dwelling on the roof of the unit below. Every five floors at the center of the building, a pedestrian walkway threads through, running from one elevator core to the other. Each alternating vertical wall is doubled to accommodate, within it, access stairs to the unit. Whereas some units are entered directly off the pedestrian street, others are accessed through the stairs, never more than two floors above or below the street. Units can also be two-story-high duplexes. They can occupy the full width of 30 feet, from one structural wall to the other, and range in size from 600 square feet to 2,400 square feet or more, with almost limitless variety. As an option, a nonstructural subfloor can be installed above the structural slab, thus giving full flexibility to placement of kitchens, bathrooms, air-conditioning, and data distribution. Also, the subfloor detail allows for the effective waterproofing of the roof garden, as the floating deck facilitates roofing drainage while maintaining level continuity for indoor and outdoor spaces.

In this concept there is greater variation in quality of the environment offered within the dwellings than at Habitat '67. Some houses project dramatically out of the building envelope, maximizing exposure to light and air; others recede deeper into the building, producing a shadier environment that balances out with superior exposure to the rear-window face of the structure. Most apartments are generously endowed with daylight, with windows possible on the average of two faces and partially on the side faces of the dwelling.

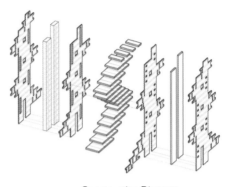

Construction Diagram

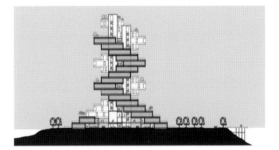

Section

Rendering of Study Number 1

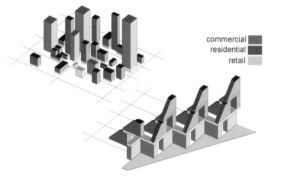

commercial ■
residential ■
retail ■

Urban Comparison Diagram,
Traditional (top) and Study Number 2

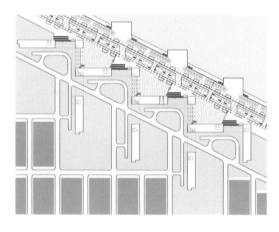

Ground Floor Plan

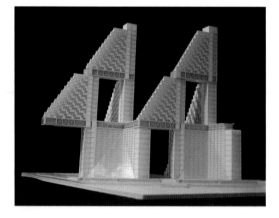

Model

Study Number 2
URBAN WINDOW HABITAT

Like Study #1, Study #2 consists of vertically stacked buildings and structural systems in vertical modules of twenty stories. The individual slab buildings, sometimes rectangular, sometimes stepped to form roof terraces, are stacked corner to corner and can accommodate offices, hotels, or residences. As these slabs are stacked vertically, trusses allow for the slabs to span from core to core, forming large-scale, 150-feet-wide by 240-feet-high "urban windows." The resulting mass is exceedingly porous, framing views of city and sky and providing open views from within.

Assuming a linear site along an urban edge, a riverfront, a seashore, or a great park, the complex would be organized along a pedestrian street accommodating shops and community facilities. We have developed such a model for the Marina Bay Sands complex in Singapore. The first layer of slabs would primarily be office space: two slabs form an L-shaped structure joined by a glazed atrium and connecting to the pedestrian urban spine. At the twentieth floor, a secondary community pedestrian street traverses the entire complex in trusses that span the lower office blocks. Community-related facilities are clustered along this route. A second and third stack of slabs, primarily residential, complete the project to its height of a total of sixty floors. The density achieved is formidable, yet the urban windows, as well as the terraced massing of the residential slab, provide for openness, views, and generous daylight, with multiple orientations. Approximately half the units in the complex are provided with gardens open to the sky; others are compensated with solariums, bay windows, and balconies.

The extraordinary achievement here is the reliance on completely traditional, vertically stacked slab towers, with the exception of the trusses that enable them to span from core to core. This means conventional construction and structures, plumbing, building services, and vertically stacked elevators are placed with great efficiency, and fire-exiting and safety schemes are both effective and efficient. The building economics of such a proposal are familiar and predictable, yet the level of amenity offered greatly exceeds that of traditional mixed-use complexes of similar densities.

Compared to the amenities of Habitat '67, undoubtedly this scheme does not provide as consistent, as generous, or as private accommodations. On the other hand, it promises to be exceedingly more affordable and capable of application to a great variety of urban development sites today.

Study Number 3

UNDULATING MEMBRANE HABITAT

One of the features of the unbuilt Habitat proposal was its formation on hill-like "membranes." These were structures with housing terracing downwards but hollow from behind. Thus, the seemingly floating membranes provided for terracing open to the sky with apartments that opened in two and sometimes three directions. As in a hill town, alleys or walkways occurred every three, four, or five levels, traversing horizontally along the contours served at the ends by vertical or inclined elevators. In the original Habitat proposal, the membranes were supported by structural A-frames at each end, which also accommodated an inclined elevator system. (Such elevators are today a standard off-the-shelf product, but more costly and slower.) While membranes provided the rich amenities of hillside living, the structural liabilities of an inclined structure with economic consequences were considerable.

In response, we have developed two variations of membrane hillside housing. The first membrane warps from a gently inclined plane to a vertical one, undulating into a second cycle inclining in the opposite direction. Thus the warped surface, sixteen-stories high, goes through the transition of inclined to vertical and again inclined. The vertical juncture point in the membrane is where a core of vertical elevators and fire stairs is located. Though there is a variable degree of inclination forming terraces and roof gardens, the structure itself is self-stiffening, self-supporting, and served by traditional vertical cores.

To minimize the impact of the membrane inclination, the floor slabs at each level, working in tandem with columns of variable inclination, are braced on the underside of the membrane by a diagrid — or diagonal grid — structure that spans between the vertical cores. This helps support the horizontal thrust forces, minimizing the structural liability of the inclined membrane. An undulating, wavelike public promenade caps the roof and serves as a community public garden. A system of horizontal pedestrian streets traverses the structure every five floors and, in a manner similar to Studies #1 and #2, leads to apartments either one or two floors up or down from the main street level. The street level, having been placed on the outer face, benefits from daylight and dramatic views.

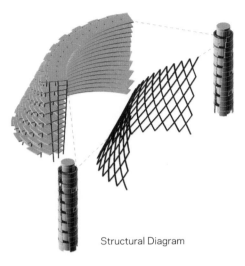

Structural Diagram

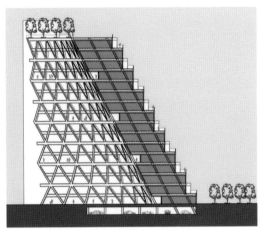

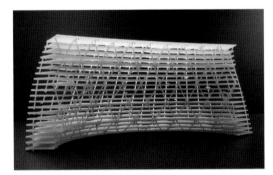

Section

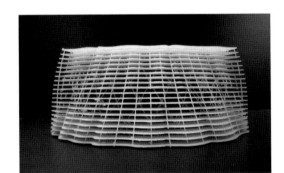

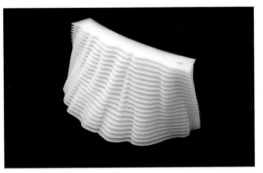

Study Models

Rendering of Study Number 2

Rendering of Study Number 3

Study Number 4
A-FRAME MEMBRANE HABITAT

One of the weaknesses of Study #3 is that the undulating membrane structure forms a wall-like element in the urban landscape. This wall of building mass does not allow for open-view corridors. These are needed to mitigate the wall-like syndrome, particularly when development occurs along scenic routes, such as beaches and major parks. While recognizing the inferior overall economics of an A-frame membrane structure, we pursued a study in which the original, unbuilt Habitat design is modified to be structurally more efficient by varying both the geometry and the structural system from the original. The "rhomboid" of the unbuilt Habitat was changed into curved membranes supported on each side by A-frames. These frames accommodate inclined elevators and fire stairs. Floor slabs, inclined columns, and diagrids make up the structure as in Study #3.

Large urban windows — dramatic gaps or openings — are made possible within the porous building. The structural efficiencies, direct plumbing lines, and reduced building envelope all make this scheme considerably more economical than the original Habitat design. It also creates flexible loft spaces that can be constructed at will by residents into any combination of dwelling sizes.

Rendering of Study Number 4

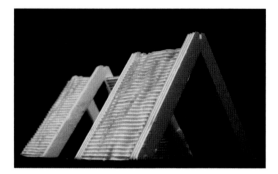

Study Model

Elevation Rendering

Study Number 5

STACKED MEMBRANES HABITAT

The original Habitat design from 1964 proposed housing "membranes" shaped as rhomboids supported by A-frames as the basic housing structure. The prefabricated modules were stacked in spiral formations, inclined and supported by a network of pedestrian streets acting as lateral beams, in turn supported by A-frames. As they leaned back against each other, large land areas were sheltered under these membranes, partially open to the sky and partially covered by the housing. Parking structures, community shopping, schools, and some offices were integrated into this lower-level base.

For the central urban areas of great metropolitan cities, however, the demand for greater densities prevails. As a strategy for increasing density, the concept of stacking office towers topped by residential development emerged. Layering offices with housing above helps achieve triple densities without serious compromise to the quality of life provided at the upper-level housing, particularly in terms of views and sunlight.

In Study #2 this layering is achieved by office and housing "slabs" stacked vertically, made possible by bridge trusses spanning from core to core. Could a similar density be accomplished by deploying inclined membranes for the upper housing component spanning atop office towers? Study #5 endeavors to achieve this. From the base of a linear pedestrian spine accommodating retail and community facilities (as well as parking) rises a series of office slabs to a height of twenty-five floors. The office slabs are connected at their roof by a continuous "community street," which spans from tower to tower. Rising above are inclined residential structures contained by A-frames, which are supported by the office slabs and their elevator cores. The pedestrian bridges, which span from tower to tower, tie the structure together into a stable whole and resist the lateral forces created by the inclined buildings. Thus, hillside membranes of terraced housing rise above the office towers, leaning against each other, achieving high densities while leaving the ground level open for parks and recreation.

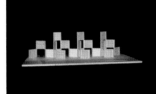
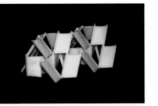

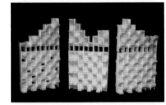

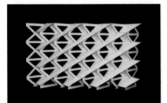
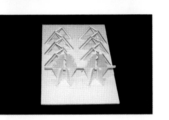

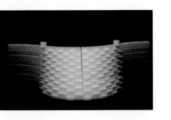
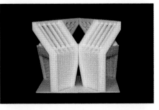

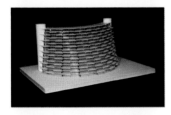

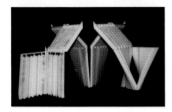

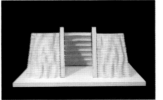

Study Models

Models of Study Number 5

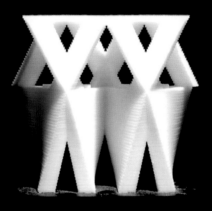

Preliminary Rendering of
Study Number 5

Balcony Renderings of
Study Number 5

CONCLUSION: HABITAT AND BEYOND

The studies carried out through 2007–2008 reveal a great diversity of issues—density, geography, and building technologies—that profoundly affect the investigation of future projects. Certain common themes are worth noting as tentative conclusions.

Mixed Use: As we explore greater densities of urban development, the advantages of mixed uses—office-employment space, residences, commercial development, and community services—become apparent. Specifically, the vertical layering of office space and residential development makes increasing density possible, while achieving optimal massing and daylight for the residences.

Stacking of uses also suggests that bridging high-rise structures at intermittent levels enables horizontal communication, enhances security and mobility, and can lead to the creation of community amenities of great quality, open to dramatic views of the city.

There is a threshold of increasing complexity between structures that fundamentally remain vertically stacked, deploying traditional vertical elevators and structures, and those that are inclined, twisted, or terraced. This becomes particularly acute as the height of buildings increases beyond twenty-five floors.

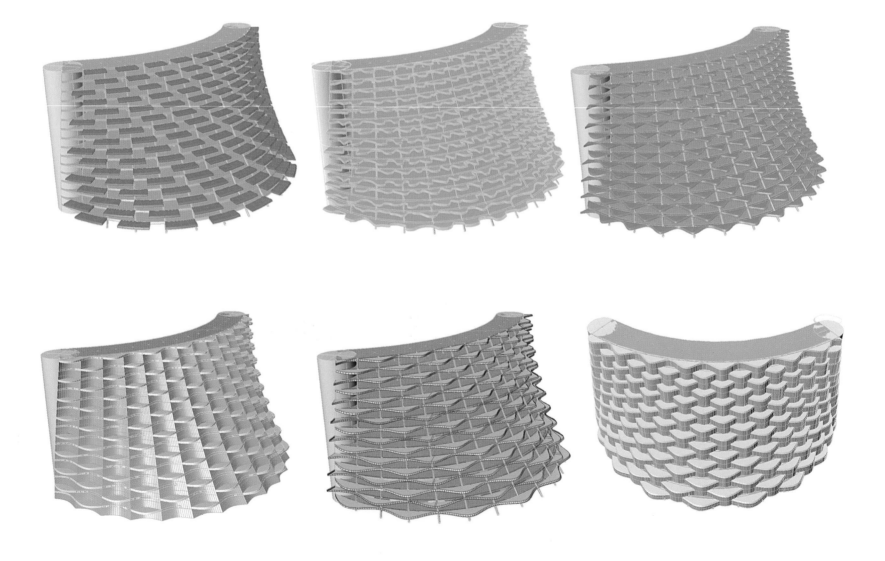

Fractalization: The more we break up the building mass, the greater potential for roof terraces and multiple orientations for every dwelling. In fact, the porosity of the mass helps to psychologically mitigate density. On the other hand, fractalization increases surface area, with a resulting impact on energy consumption and construction economics. The studies indicate the need to find a balance between adequate exposures for the dwelling without overstretching the building envelope. This balance fluctuates from climate to climate, with the severe colder climates presenting a greater constraint to fractalization than tropical ones.

Orientation: The Habitat studies of 1967, developed for a Montreal setting with its particularly severe winter climate, recognized the ideal of southern orientation to maximize exposure to sun in winter and transitional seasons. The original unbuilt Habitat concept comprised housing membranes sloping towards the southeast and southwest, achieving a uniform optimization of this idealized orientation for all dwellings. In contrast to the original scheme, Habitat '67, as constructed with three twelve-story clusters, compromised this ideal. Units were oriented towards the city and river, varying orientation from southeast-southwest to include northern exposure.

The current studies demonstrate the difficulty of achieving standardized orientation. Certain sites and certain building arrangements, which may have many geometric structural advantages, end up compromising on orientation.

It is an open question whether a consistent orientation is relevant in all climates. Certainly, in the tropics and other typically hot climates, cross-ventilation might take a priority, though western orientation can be problematic. Similarly, housing membranes that shade public spaces at the ground level can have great advantages in tropical climates, while being potentially oppressive through the winters of colder climate zones.

Building Technology: The verdict is not yet in on the optimization of construction technology for highrise residential development. The concept of three-dimensional modules prefinished in the factory, embraced for the original Habitat, has proven its limitations. The conflict between the size of shippable modules and the size of dwellings has meant that only part of the dwelling unit can be prefabricated. Even the joining of two or three trailer houses to form one unit demonstrates the technical difficulties entailed.

The shift has been to deploy different structural frames, either steel or concrete, creating floor plates which are then finished and enclosed more traditionally. Pre-made modules, such as bathrooms, kitchens, and other residential components, can still be used and are subject to further development. There have been technological advances in prefabricating the building skin as well. However, what we have not yet seen in the construction industry are lightweight, fireproof materials, capable of bearing loads, that can replace the concrete boxes of Habitat.

The rationalization of the building process for residential development is therefore yet unclear. It remains field- and labor-intensive, subject to endless corrective actions during construction, all to be once more modified as residents shape their dwellings in their own image.

Finally, in response to the question of "why Habitat has not proliferated," it is important to note the continued tension between desire and resources. As we have seen in recent years, the super-luxury housing that occurs in many cities often seeks to create the amenities similar to those provided in Habitat. The line of desire, therefore, remains constant. One must conclude that the concept of Habitat is an idea whose time is yet to come.

**SAFDIE ARCHITECTS
RESEARCH FELLOWSHIP**

Fellowship Coordinator:
Christopher Mulvey

Habitat of the Future
Project Director:
Lorenzo Mattii

Project Team:
James Forren
Eleanor Kebabian
Michael Shur

GOING FORWARD

HUMANIZING MEGASCALE AND THE PUBLIC REALM

Moshe Safdie

On the Occasion of the Conferring of the
2015 American Institute of Architects Gold Medal

President Clinton, AIA President Elizabeth Chu Richter, dear family, friends, and colleagues:

President Clinton – I am deeply moved that this event is graced by your presence. You were present at the inauguration of the Rabin Center in Tel Aviv and of Crystal Bridges Museum of American Art in Arkansas.

I am deeply honored to receive this award, particularly as it is bestowed by my peers. I do so with humility, combined with a sense of confidence, that it represents a recognition of the ideals and principles that have guided my work as an architect for the past fifty years.

As for humility, I always tell my students that if every time they take a pencil in hand to design – if they can identify completely with those who will live, work, and be in their building, it is half the way to victory.

I was born into a state in the making. It was an idealistic moment in my people's history. It was not driven by fanaticism of religion, but by the ideology of the Enlightenment. I grew up in the time of the kibbutz, the cooperatives – a society that believed in equity.

This experience had profound impact, forming my being as an architect in relationship to society. I do not say this as an abstraction, but rather from the perspective of where I (may I say we) stood in relationship to those whom we served.

Ideals translate into an ethic, an ethic that must guide us as a profession. It is for each of us to personally figure out, but what more fitting moment today for me to declare my own.

I reflect on the words of my mentor, Louis Kahn: "Let a building be what it wants to be." What is a building's inherent and deep purpose? To me, it is discovering the life intended in a building, be it a school, hospital, performing arts center, airport, or mosque.

If you design a school, one question matters: Is it a conducive place for learning? This exploration for fitness to purpose must be at the center of architectural invention!

As a profession, designing the physical environment, we draw heavily on society's resources. Our art is a material one. How we use materials – the building systems we evolve, the energy our buildings consume – is fundamental to a responsible building.

This is about designing buildings that are inherently buildable, which are conceived, to use Frank Lloyd Wright's words, "…in the nature of materials." This is what differentiates us from the other arts – from sculpture, from music. Through generations, it has been a powerful component of architectural expression.

We were all here born into a globalizing world. My commissions have drawn me to every continent and many countries and cultures. I have had the good fortune to design places for the Inuits in the Arctic, the peasants of West Africa, places for Sikhs and Muslims, national institutions for Canada, US, Israel, and China.

I became an attentive student of culture. I discovered the satisfaction of creating buildings which truly belong, which feel as if they had always been there, yet responding and resonating to the needs of today.

I learned that architecture cannot be independent of place, and the notion that there are universal solutions that fit all must disappear as Colonialism did. All-glass skyscrapers in the desert were not meant to be, any more than igloos in the tropics.

I've always believed that we must draw on our heritage, the lessons learned from those who built before us. In the words of Ecclesiastes: "There is nothing new under the sun." Without contradicting the scriptures, it is also true that there is always the challenge of the moment: a planet in which, now, the great majority live in cities.

In the countryside and towns, we had guaranteed open space, air, light and contact with nature. Now living in cities, whose size escapes our imagination – 10, 20, 30 million and growing, and at densities that were not intended for a species which evolved roaming the Savannahs.

The reality is of a world in which the dominant building type is the high-rise building. With it, life's sustaining elements are threatened: light, air, a sense of identity, contact with nature, privacy, as well as community. Neither the privacy of a house, nor the community of a village, are possible now without major new inventions which transcend individual buildings. They demand a new urban vision.

I have always felt that this should be the American Institute of Architects and Urbanists. In every age, and in every school of architectural thought, architectural concepts were derived from concepts of the city as a whole.

Architects always recognized that it is the aggregation of buildings that form places, and places form districts, and districts form cities. It is the urban environment that we experience in our daily life that really matters. At a time where our cities are both thriving and ailing, proliferating to accommodate the majority of humankind, yet increasingly depriving us from the fundamental qualities of life, not only light, air, and nature, but the deprivation of mobility; the erosion and privatization of the public realm; now is the time to declare, once again, that it is the cities we create that really matter.

And since we are in Atlanta, may I dare echo – "I have a dream." I have a dream of high-rise cities transformed, penetrated by light and sun, with plant life and gardens on land and sky. Towers clustered into communities, served by innovative modes of transportation, mobility restored.

That the Agora, Souk, and city squares of bygone days are reinvented into new centers, integrating culture, commerce, and governance into places we can call an urban oasis. Where privatized malls give way to vital and inclusive city centers worthy of our civilization.

Humanizing megascale is the single most urgent task that awaits us in the decades to come.

In accepting this award I want to remind us that making architecture is a collective act. Like grand opera, it takes a composer, libretto writer, conductor, chorus master, soloists, and many others to achieve.

I thank the devoted members of my firm, many there for decades. I thank the brilliant engineers and other specialists I have had the good fortune to collaborate with, and, last but not least, the committed clients who have made all this possible.

Thirty years ago, concluding my book *Form & Purpose*, I summed up my thoughts in a poem. What I wrote then seems relevant today:

He who seeks truth shall find beauty.

He who seeks beauty shall find vanity.

He who seeks order shall find gratification.

He who seeks gratification shall be disappointed.

He who considers himself the servant of his fellow beings shall find
     the joy of self-expression.

He who seeks self-expression shall fall into the pit of arrogance.

Arrogance is incompatible with nature.

Through nature, the nature of the universe and the nature of man,
     we shall seek truth.

If we seek truth, we shall find beauty.

Moshe Safdie
Atlanta, Georgia
May 14, 2015

Marina Bay Sands, Singapore

Raffles City, Chongqing, China

Jewel at Changi, Changi Airport, Singapore

A citizen of the world in both practice and in the essence of his work, which celebrates people and place, respecting and enriching the cultures in which his genius interacts. A visionary, his projects transcend time and fashion with a clarity and joy in making that lift the eye and celebrate the spirit. Gifted teacher, inspired and inspiring mentor, apostle of beauty whose art reimagines the classic geometry of form-making with an invigorating modern spirit, he gives voice to the prose of the earth's materials and teaches stone, glass, and steel to sing.

AIA GOLD MEDAL CITATION, 2015

"Memory, creativity: the linkage of these two ideas
is the cornerstone of the Skirball Cultural Center."

Herbert Muschamp
New York Times
December 15, 1996

Skirball Cultural Center

LOS ANGELES, CALIFORNIA

A Photographic Portfolio

Acknowledgments

The *Global Citizen* exhibition, along with its catalogue and traveling installation, is the result of the creativity, talent, and dedicated work of many individuals. I would like to thank Alice Walton, founder, Crystal Bridges Museum of American Art, and Uri D. Herscher, founding president and chief executive officer, Skirball Cultural Center, who together initiated this ambitious project. Of the many staff members involved at Crystal Bridges, I specifically want to acknowledge the ongoing efforts of Elizabeth Weinman Miller, registrar. At the Skirball, thanks go to Robert Kirschner, museum director, Cynthia Tovar, registrar, and Kathryn Girard, chief of staff. Coordination of aspects of this complex exhibition on behalf of the Crystal Bridges Museum was skillfully carried out by David A. Hanks & Associates: David A. Hanks; Jan L. Spak, project manager; and Kate Clark, administrative assistant. Liora Cobin preformed superb research, and Natalie W. Shivers offered expert advice and editing on my essay and the exhibition and catalogue text. It has also been a pleasure to work with the staffs of the National Gallery of Canada, the National Academy Museum in New York, and the Boston Society of Architects.

We had the good fortune to work with some very creative individuals whose contributions were vital to the success of the exhibition. The design of the exhibition, which presents the architecture of Moshe Safdie from a new perspective, was the collaborative effort of a talented team. Nader Tehrani, Remon Alberts, and Yewona Chun of Office dA (now NADAAA) designed the exhibition installations; Pure+Applied created the exhibition graphics (as well as the exhibition catalogue); Charles Maltbie, Jr. and the staff of Maltbie fabricated all the installation components; and Duncan Swain oversaw the restoration of the Habitat bathroom. And, finally, Arnold + Arnold Architectural Scale Models and Bohai Models skillfully fabricated new models for the exhibition.

Sarah Williams Goldhagen's essay analyzes Moshe Safdie's work and reviews it in the context of contemporary architectural practice. Gus Powell's engaging, newly commissioned photo essay of the Salt Lake City Public Library utilized in the exhibition and catalogue reveals the interaction of people and architecture. Thanks also go to Maurice Linnane of Long Grass Productions for his film of the National Gallery of Canada that so eloquently conveys Safdie's architecture as it is experienced through social ritual and ceremony.

Great thanks are due to the lenders to the exhibition, including Crystal Bridges Museum of American Art, Bentonville, Arkansas; Khalsa Heritage Centre, Anandpur Sahib Foundation, Chandigarh, India; Hebrew Union College-Jewish Institute of Religion, Jerusalem, Israel; Peabody Essex Museum, Salem, Massachusetts; Safdie Architects, Somerville, Massachusetts; Moshe Safdie Archive, McGill University, Montreal, Quebec; and the Skirball Cultural Center, Los Angeles, California. We wish to particularly recognize the McGill University Library, the repository of the Safdie archives, and especially Ann Marie Holland, archivist. Irena Murray, Linda Grief, and Julie Korman helped make the Safdie archive available for research. And for the conservation of the McGill drawings, we appreciate the excellent work of Cartgo Services Muséologiques, in particular Yasmée Faucher and Josée Noël.

For their enthusiasm and expertise in producing this exhibition catalogue, we are indebted to the following at Scala Publishers: Jennifer Wright Norman, director of publications; Stephanie Emerson, project manager and copyeditor; Oliver Craske, editorial director; and Tim Clarke, production director. Their commitment to the project and attention to detail brought the catalogue to fruition.

Credit must be given to the staff of Safdie Architects, specifically: Peppi Dotan, Christa Mahar, Christopher Mulvey, Sarah Perz, Greg Reaves, and Juan Villafane, and the members of the model shop led by Anthony DePace, all of whom contributed knowledge and diligently gathered key information for the exhibition and catalogue. The staff fulfilled a myriad of tasks, from making available models and drawings to providing architectural photographs. Finally, I personally, and all the people involved with this project, are deeply grateful to Moshe Safdie for his extraordinary efforts and his insights on architecture — and much more.

Donald Albrecht
Exhibition curator and catalogue editor

Notes

Donald Albrecht

1.   Jefferson Graham, "Here's America's Unquietest Library," *USA Today*, October 14, 2003.
     The library's populist coverage included providing the setting of a 2006 issue of the *Archie*
     comic book.

2.   Moshe Safdie, "On Ethics, Order and Complexity," the architect's essay in *Moshe Safdie II*
     (Victoria, Australia: The Images Publishing Group, 2009), 8.

3.   Moshe Safdie, quoted in Beth Kapusta, "Canada's Master of the Popular Gesture," Toronto *Globe and Mail*, April 26,
     1997. For an extensive analysis of the Vancouver Library Square, including its controversial reception, see the special
     issue of *Architecture in Canada* 25, no. 1, 2000.

4.   The tour was sponsored by a Canadian Mortgage and Housing Corporation Traveling Scholarship.

5.   Safdie discusses the concept of three-dimensional communities in his book *For Everyone a Garden* (Cambridge, Mass.,
     and London: The MIT Press, 1974).

6.   Ada Louise Huxtable, "Habitat: Exciting Concept, Flawed Execution," *New York Times*, April 30, 1967.

7.   Safdie's Ardmore Habitat (1980–85) in Singapore compressed the Habitat concept into two seventeen-story towers.

8.   Moshe Safdie, quoted in Witold Rybczynski, "With Wear and Tear, Habitat Has Become a Home," *New York Times*,
     August 5, 1990.

9.   Ibid.

10. Moshe Safdie, quoted in Carolyn Skaug, "Still No Plans on Union," *Phoenix*, October 9, 1969.

11. Reginald H. Biggs, telegram to the San Francisco State College Board of Trustees, September 26, 1968, Archives of
     San Francisco State College.

12. *For Everyone a Garden*, 332.

13. Moshe Safdie, *Form & Purpose* (Boston: Houghton Mifflin Co., 1982), 43.

14. *Form & Purpose*, 107. Historic Jerusalem was the subject of two books derived from Safdie's teaching at Harvard:
     The Harvard-Jerusalem Studio: Urban Designs for the Holy City (Cambridge, Mass.: The MIT Press and Israel:
     Keterpress Enterprises, 1986) and *Jerusalem: The Future of the Past* (Boston: Houghton Mifflin Co., 1989).
     Additionally, in 1989, the Harvard University Graduate School of Design published *The Language and Medium
     of Architecture* based on one of Safdie's lectures.

15. Esther Zandberg, "If Herod Built a Disco," *Ha'aretz* (English edition), December 17, 1998.

16. Moshe Safdie, quoted in David B. Green, "Herod's Successor," *The Jerusalem Report*, September 18, 1999, 42.

17. Esther Zandberg, quoted in Eric Siblin, "Peace Work," *Saturday Night* [Toronto], October 21, 2000, 50.

18. Martin Peretz, "An Architectural Triumph. Memory Palace," *The New Republic*, April 18, 2005, 17.

19. Moshe Safdie, quoted in Corinna Da Fonseca-Wollheim, "Sacred Ground, Sullied Ground," *New York Times*,
     May 10, 2005.

20. Moshe Safdie, quoted in Julia M. Klein, "He's a Revisionist Modernist," *Wall Street Journal*, August 29, 2007.

21. "If Herod Built a Disco."

22. Campbell summarized his position on the city's role in the project with his article's headline, "New York: Quick Cash,
     Bad Planning," *Boston Globe*, September 8, 1987.

23. Moshe Safdie, quoted in "He's a Revisionist Modernist."

24. Other key Canadian buildings include the Quebec Museum of Civilization in Quebec City (1981–87), the Montreal
     Museum of Fine Arts (1985–91), the Ottawa City Hall (1988–94), the Vancouver Library Square (1992–95), and the
     Ford Center for the Performing Arts in Vancouver (1994–95).

25. John F. Burns, "For Canada's Art, A Home of Its Own," *New York Times*, May 21, 1988.

26. Anthony Lewis, "Reason to Celebrate," *New York Times*, May 26, 1988.

27. Moshe Safdie, quoted in "Sacred Ground, Sullied Ground."

28. Directed by Clayton Farr and produced by Global Artways, the film is entitled *Community Building: The Creation of a Modern Public Library* and is available as a DVD.

29. "He's a Revisionist Modernist."

30. These quotes are from Moshe Safdie's description of the mosque in an office project description, dated May 2008.

31. "On Ethics, Order and Complexity."

32. Moshe Safdie, with Wendy Kohn, *The City After the Automobile: An Architect's Vision* (Toronto: Stoddart Publishing Co., 1997), 3.

33. Ibid., 89.

34. Ibid., 90. Koolhaas's quotes come from *S,M,L,XL: Small, Medium, Large, Extra-Large*, written with Bruce Mau and published by The Monacelli Press, New York, in 1995.

35. "On Ethics, Order and Complexity."

36. *The City After the Automobile*, 91.

Sarah Williams Goldhagen

In researching and writing this essay I have used numerous sources, most notably Moshe Safdie's own writings, which are cited in Donald Albrecht's essay in this book, and a podcast of a lecture Safdie delivered at McGill University in Montreal, which is available on the university's Moshe Safdie Hypermedia Archive (http://cac.mcgill.ca/safdie). Also valuable were Alison Smithson (editor), *Team 10 Primer* (Cambridge, Mass.: The MIT Press, 1968); the Team 10 website (www.team10online.org); and Eric Mumford's *Defining Urban Design: CIAM Architects and the Formation of a Discipline, 1937–1969* (New Haven, Conn.: Yale University Press, 2009). For further background, readers are advised to consult two of my own publications: *Louis Kahn's Situated Modernism* (New Haven, Conn.: Yale University Press, 2001) and "The Production of Locality in Josep Lluís Sert's Peabody Terrace," published in the Fall 2005/Winter 2006 issue of *Harvard Design Magazine*.

Moshe Safdie

1.   Moshe Safdie, *For Everyone a Garden* (Cambridge, Mass.: The MIT Press, 1974).

Index

Page numbers in italics refer to illustrations.

Photo Credits

© Canada Post Corporation (2007). Reproduced with
permission: 37 below

Photographs by John Horner: 40, 41 left and above
right, 43 below

Photographs by Timothy Hursley: front cover, 37 above,
46–49, 56–67, 72–75, 81–84, 91, 96 below,
97, 107 below, 132–3, 136–137, 151

Louis I. Kahn Collection, University of Pennsylvania
and the Pennsylvania Historical and Museum
Commission: 99 above

Photographs © Alan Karchmer: 68–71

Courtesy of Moshe Safdie Archive, John Bland
Canadian Architecture Collection, McGill
University Library, Montreal, Canada:
31 center, 34–35, 38–39, 98

Photograph by Grant Mudford: 146 above

From *Newsweek*, April 19, 1971 © 1971 Newsweek,
Inc. All rights reserved. Used by permission and
protected by the Copyright Laws of the United
States. The printing, copying, redistribution, or
retransmission of the Material without express
written permission is prohibited: 30 left

Photograph by Frank Pinckers: p. 134

Photographs by Gus Powell, © 2007 by Gus Powell:
2–19, 93 below, 149

Photographs © Ram Rahman: 42, 76–77, 95 above

Courtesy of Safdie Architects: 28, 29, 31 above,
31 below, 90, 92, 93 above, 94, 95 below,
96 above and center, 99 below, 107 below,
108–109, 112–113, 122–126, 138–142,
Back Cover; created by Archpartners: 41 below
right, 110–111, 114–121; © Crystal CG: 43
above

Photographs by Michal Ronnen Safdie: 32, 36, 52–55,
78–79

Courtesy of Skirball Cultural Center, photographs by
Alex Vertikoff: 146 below, 147; by Tim Schirtz:
148; by John Elder: 150, 152–3

Photographs by Jerry Spearman: 30 right, 107 above

Photograph by Studio Graetz: 50–51